MW01173913

Earn a PhD in Sales

In

5 B.A.S.I.C. Steps

John R. Landrine

Copyright ©2016 John R. Landrine
All Rights Reserved.
ISBN-13:978-1530188406
ISBN-10: 1530188407

To My Fellow Sales Professionals
And Mentors

I dedicate this book to those who have been the foundation of my education and the source of my inspiration. To those who have helped form the pillars of my core beliefs and my understanding of the world of selling. To those whose example of professionalism, honesty, integrity, and quality, as well as their demonstration of motivation, perseverance and determination has shaped and guided my career; to you all, I gratefully and humbly thank you.

To Wesley Bates who showed me the meaning of persistence and Lloyd Allard who defined the consummate professional. To Sean McPheat, Zig Ziglar and Jim Rohn for the never ending supply of sophisticated, yet practical training material.

To those peers and partners whom I have had the honor to work with like John Mauriello, Richard Hemma, Rupee Atwal and posthumously, my dear friend Charlie Jones.

And to all of you that I have had the opportunity to share some insight into this, the greatest of all occupations, I thank you for contributing so much to a wonderful, joyful and blessed career.

God Bless You!

John R. Landrine

Earn a PhD in Sales
In
5 B.A.S.I.C Steps

Table of Contents

"This is one of the most important books ever written for professional sales people."

Whether you have been in sales for 30 days or 30 years, you need to read this book and make these 5 BASIC principles the foundation of your career. "Earn a PhD. in Sales in 5 BASIC Steps" will show you how to operate on the level of one with a doctorate in the business. Raise your professionalism to the PhD. level and you'll raise your income to levels you never thought were possible."

---Sean McPheat
Founder and Managing Director of MTD Sales Training,

"Uplifting and exhilarating; this book will give you a fresh and renewed sense of pride and enthusiasm in the world of selling."

"Earn a PhD in Sales is uplifting and motivational, yet very technical. You will learn some of the most advanced techniques and strategies in the business and a hundred ways to help you get better at what you do. You will walk away from this book with a feeling and sense of pride that you've never had before. You will say, "I AM A SALES PROFESSIONAL," with the sense of dignity of a Supreme Court Judge.

---Wesley Bates
GM National Auto Club

i

Earn a PhD in Sales
In
5 B.A.S.I.C Steps

Foreword
By Wesley Bates

I cannot think of a more appropriate title for this book. I, for one, have always felt that true professional sales people need some sort of degree or distinguishing label or title that instantly proclaims one who is at the top of their field.

Lord knows, there are dozens of labels for those sales people who are less than honest, slip-shod, and unprofessional but who operate in the name of professional selling, all the while tarnishing the name and image of the greatest profession in the world. I salute you, John!

Over the course of this book, you are going to learn some of the most powerful and advanced sales tips, techniques and philosophies that you have ever heard of, from my friend and world-renowned sales superstar and trainer, John Landrine.

John will indeed share some concepts and ideas with you that can transform your sales career, take you to the next level, and all the way to the point of holding a PhD in sales. However, there is one caveat that I wanted to mention to every reader of this book; there is one catch. The catch is that this is going require some WORK!

If you are someone looking for a quick fix or some instantaneous formula that will suddenly transform your sales career, you are looking in the wrong place.

I am sorry to tell you, but in this book, you will not find a new super pitch, some magical scripts, or any prospect brainwashing tips. However, you will find valuable, practical and proven information from someone who has been there and done everything that you will read here.

Some of you may not have heard of John Landrine before and that is because he has spent the last 15 years of his illustrious sales career *behind the scenes*. John works with some of the largest and most successful sales companies and training organizations in the world, providing them with training and advice, mostly from a "ghost" position. John is the professional ghostwriter behind more articles, books and sales material than you can imagine. Chances are that you have read some of John's material somewhere at some time. So, let me take this opportunity to tell you a little bit about John R. Landrine.

John began his sales career at the tender age of just nine years old when he was living in the rough, gang-ridden, drug infested East Falls Projects in West Philadelphia, PA. Raised by a single parent, John and his siblings struggled in very poor conditions, as his mother did the best that she could to keep food on the table.

Always looking for ways that he could contribute to the household and be *the man of the house,* John had been thinking about the local Girl Scout troops and how, when they came through the neighborhoods, they would always sell tons of boxes of cookies. John imagined that those girls probably generated a ton of money. Having an inborn mind for business and the heart and spirit of an entrepreneur, John decided to start his own candy business.

One day John *borrowed* $1 from his mother. He used thirty-five cents to board a city bus that he rode for over an hour, out to a nice, upscale area far from the projects where he lived. He walked into the nearest supermarket, and after a short survey of the cookies and candy isle; he purchased one box of *Sophia Mae Peanut Brittle* for fifty cents. He then bought a big brown-paper shopping bag for a nickel.

With the remaining ten cents, John remembered that his mother had told him that no matter what, always keep a dime to call home in case of an emergency (and always to wear clean underwear in case of that emergency as well). Since he was some thirty or forty miles away from home and had no transportation or money, he did exactly as his mom instructed and tucked the precious, possibly life-saving, coin deep down into his right sock.

John walked around the corner from the supermarket, and made the very first *cold call* he had ever made by knocking on the first door he came to. When the woman opened the door, John went into the very first sales presentation he ever delivered.

An extremely honest young man, John felt that his selling candy would not only help him earn a little bit of money to help his mom, but he also knew that it would help him stay out of trouble in the dangerous streets that had consumed the lives of so many young men of color. John felt that by working hard all day (and he knew that going door-to-door all day long was definitely hard work) that it would help him avoid the drugs and gangs that permeated the community, constantly smothering lives and destroying the futures of too many children and adults.

So his presentation was nothing more than the simple truth, as he explained that he was selling candy to earn a little money and stay out of the gangs and drugs in the streets. People knew that they could buy the same candy down the street at the supermarket for a third of the cost, but most empathized with this young industrious little entrepreneur and wanted to help. Not only did people receive good, fresh merchandise, but they also got an injection of warm and fuzzy pride and gratification for having helped the little, disadvantaged kid.

The woman at the first door was happy to contribute to the *cause* and gladly paid John the $1.50 that he was asking for the box of candy, and she gave him a fifty-cent tip.

John ran back to the store with the $2 and bought four boxes of the peanut brittle, and he sold those. He went back and forth like that all day, each time increasing his inventory and then completely selling it out. By the end of a very long and hard day, John finally dragged himself onto the bus heading home and collapsed in a seat, exhausted. John had tired aching feet, sweaty musty clothes, a huge smile on his face and over $87 dollars in his pocket!

Because he had to go school, he wasn't able to work and sell candy every day. However, during the summer months, John often averaged a net of about $400 a week. In 1968, $400, adjusted for inflation, at the time of this writing comes out to about $2,790 a week, which was no small piece of change for a 9-year old kid.

Over the ensuing years, John's door-to-door candy business grew as he knocked on literally thousands of doors and conducted tens of thousands of sales interactions. Gaining such experience, valuable sales knowledge and practice at such a young age, led this young prodigy to become a superstar in his first professional sales position with Kirby Vacuum Cleaners, which is where John and I first met.

As the sales manager of a Kirby Vacuum Distributorship in Elmsford, New York, I was blessed with the opportunity to meet and recruit this young hotshot salesman. In his first 30 days with the company, John outsold almost everyone, including his training supervisor, and this was while he did not even have a car.

At the time he joined my organization, John did not own a car. I had told him that it would be impossible to work and sell Kirbys on a straight commission basis, and survive without reliable transportation. I mean, with all of the equipment you had to lug around and the relentless door-to-door canvassing the job required, it was impossible to think that you could do it on foot.

But John said that such a thought was nonsense and that he would make enough money in his first week to buy a car. So he set out on foot, and beat out some of the most experienced sales people on our team who all drove, and within a few weeks, he bought a car, rented a great apartment *and* furnished it.

By the time he was just 20 years old, John essentially already had over 10 years of sales experience, putting him years ahead of his peers and positioning him for management opportunities almost immediately.

John had one simple philosophy back then. He felt that since he was so young and inexperienced, (although he had a thousand times more experience, knowledge and sales understanding than anyone close to his age) that he could even the playing field by working harder than anyone else did. John felt that he could outwork anyone, at least for a short period of time. He believed that no matter how good or bad his sales and closing skills, he could see more people, knock on more doors and complete more sales demonstrations than any of his peers, and he set out to do just that.

At just 24 years old, John had moved on and became one of the most successful sales people and one of the youngest Regional Sales Managers in the history of Gulf Industries Corporation, training and leading dozens of sales people to success in the process.

Over the years, John went on to literally shatter dozens of sales records at various companies in different industries. For instance, he worked with a pharmaceuticals firm that sold generic, over-the-counter drugs over the telephone to pharmacies across the U.S. The company had locations in New York, Chicago and one in Beverley Hills, California, where John worked. The company record for opening new pharmacy accounts was 4 accounts in one day, 11 in one week and 26 in one month.

On his very first day, after some training and orientation, John got on the telephone at about 1:00 in the afternoon and by the end of that day, he had opened 4 new accounts, already tying the long-held daily sales record in his first *half* day.

On his second day, his first full day of work, he opened seven new accounts, nearly doubling the daily record and tying the weekly record in just a day and a half. John went on to *average* opening 65 new accounts per month...*every* month. Mind you, the world record was 26 accounts in one month. John's *average* was 65 accounts per month. He opened nearly 300% more accounts every month than the previous national monthly record.

Over the years, John went on to become a Vice President of Sales and Marketing at NetMagic Systems and finally a CEO at ExecuTrain Corporation, all the while consulting and helping lead hundreds of sales people to success.

John has written and published hundreds of articles and been featured in several worldwide publications like Selling Power Magazine, Life Insurance Selling and Direct Marketing. Today, sales, sales management and executive training companies around the world constantly seek John's expertise and often republish his work in their magazines and on their websites and blogs.

John is also the author of the renowned sales and communications skills training course, *"How to See on the Telephone,"* which revolutionized telephone sales techniques in the 1990s. The audio-training course taught the principles of Psycholinguistics. In the course, John taught sales people, managers, executives and others how to use *tone of voice and pace of speech* over the telephone, the same way you use *facial expression and body language* in person. Selling Power Magazine said that John's course, *"Represented the most advanced telephone selling techniques ever developed..."*

Today, as an independent sales and marketing consultant and ghostwriter, John works mostly behind the scenes, helping clients all over the world with training in sales and on how to deal with today's modern, educated and internet-connected consumer. He also helps people with Christian related books.

Since the release of *How to See on the Telephone* in the 1990's, John has written and published work mostly from the position of a *ghost*; writing books, articles and other sales related material for other sales professionals, organizations and trainers.

However, over the last few years, John noticed that too many sales people today have been working harder and harder only to earn less and less. He saw that too many sales people struggle with old and out-dated techniques that do not work in today's sales environment. He realized that most sales people today simply do not understand how to deal with the educated buyer of this new age.

John also realized that not only have today's sales training and education suffered, but also the professionalism and image of the industry was at an all-time low.

He saw that today's sales landscape is littered with quick-buck artists and undertrained sales people who have no concept of the work and personal investment it takes to be a true professional.

Therefore, John decided that it was time to step back into the limelight to offer more publically available assistance to sales people around the world. John believes it is critical that we, as a professional industry, elevate the slip-shod, low threshold of performance expectations regarding what it takes to be called a "sales professional."

John believes that to be a true sales professional is not something that happens by accident or in five minutes. Becoming a professional requires years of practice, education and training.

Earn a PhD in Sales in 5 B.A.S.I.C Steps

You will find John's instruction to always be clear, simple and to the point. It will be simple, yet usually not very easy. What follows are five simple steps, or courses, if you will, that will show you exactly how to acquire the necessary experience, knowledge and skill to earn what is the equivalent of a PhD; the highest educational degree in your field. Not only can this book lead you to become a *Doctor of Selling*, it will help you to become the leading sales person in your company, among your peers and in your entire industry.

So, if you are ready to go to work and change your career and finally earn the money you deserve to earn, then it is time to get your PhD in sales!

Wesley Bates
General Manager
National Auto Club of America

INTRODUCTION

"PhD" stands for *philosophiae doctoris,* which is Latin for Doctor of Philosophy. It is the *terminal* degree or the highest degree or level of learning and education that is obtainable in a particular area of study other than medicine, law and theology.

In short, to have a PhD in any field means that you essentially know all there is to know about that subject. You are the guru, the wizard, the Grand Poobah; indeed, you are THE Doctor.

It's strange that in almost every other profession, there is some degree, some certification, some recognizable, tangible flag that signifies that the bearer has documented and proven knowledge and expertise in a certain area; but not in sales.

Yes, there are a small handful of industry specific titles and certifications, but nothing that demonstrates true sales knowledge across the board.

Imagine earning a doctorate degree in professional sales. You will quickly see that the information that is before you will elevate your understanding, experience and skill set to that level and then some.

Let me start by telling you something that I know many of you do not want to hear. What follows on these pages will indeed help you to earn the equivalent of a PhD in sales and elevate your career and consequently, your income, to levels of which you may not have ever dreamed. However, what some people may not want to hear is that this will require some real work.

It will require some hard work, and more importantly, it will take some smart work. It's going to take some tedious work; writing things down, taking notes and following direction. This will remind you of your high school or college days. Yes, I will ask you to do some studying and some homework, and yes, there will be a few quizzes; a few times where you will need to answer some questions.

To rise to another level, most sales people will need to adapt to an entirely new paradigm. You will have to change your way of thinking about what you do. You will have to change your philosophy on selling.

To do this successfully requires some effort on your part as well as some practice. It does not come naturally. You may find it difficult to change your mindset and change your current way of doing things.

After you change your thinking and your whole philosophy, after you have changed your *mind*, then you will have to change your habits. You will have to rehearse and practice doing things a different way.

It is not enough to read something, even this book, and then sit back and say, "Okay! I got it! I'm ready to be a sales superstar!" You are not going to read this book, close your eyes, then click your heels together 3 times and transform your sales career.

No. After you read this book, first, you may need to read it again. Then you need to test yourself to make sure you got it. Then you will have to complete the necessary assignments in the book and you will need to practice them to make sure that your body has it, to make sure that your habits have changed. Then you need to keep practicing so that the principles in the book become your new habits, so that it comes naturally to you. Then you will have continuing education assignments that you need to follow for the long-term. Every other high-level profession has CEs or Continuing Education credits that the person must complete to maintain their status as a professional in that industry. It should be no less for the sales profession.

Millions of sales people get some initial sales training and that's it. They never continue the learning process.

How would a medical doctor fare today if she had not read any medical information nor did anything to stay abreast with current technology and advancements in medical science since she graduated from medical school 20 years before?

Actually, in the field of medicine, that could not even happen. It is mandatory for doctors, registered nurses and other medical practitioners to maintain certain continuing education credits, taking courses and passing exams, to remain licensed to practice.

How competent could a lawyer be if he never read anything about changes to the law or studied any landmark decisions since he was in law school some 10 years before?

Examples like those seem preposterous; however, that is exactly what most sales people do. In this book, you will learn how to create a path of continuing education to ensure you keep your skills, as well as your ethical processes, up to date.

So I apologize to all of those who glanced at the title of this book and thought that they would find a quick short-list of five super-slick, one-line, golden nuggets that would instantly revitalize your sales career. Then again, you know what they say about judging a book by its cover.

Just as you are not going to become a successful brain surgeon after reading one book on brain surgery, you are not going to become a superstar sales legend after reading one book on sales; not even this one. However, if you will adhere to the principles in this book and complete the recommended assignments, and if you will adapt to the five basic philosophies and do what is required, then you will reach sales success of which most only dream.

Standards, Best Practices and Time

Again, while you will not find magical scripts and pat answers to objections in this book, you will find some very basic rules. You will find some standards, best practices and issues that you need to first understand and then adopt.

To make them clear and easy to follow, I will present those principles and practices that are the foundation to earning a PhD to you in 5 BASIC Steps.

Many of these standards and practices you will find very familiar. You will feel that you have heard many of them before or that you already practice them today. However, the key is often very subtle changes that you may not see at first. Sometimes the new information will be barely noticeable, but it is new nonetheless. This is a another one of the reasons why it will take a lot of practice, as you will have to learn to make seemingly small changes in how you do or approach some things.

Lastly, this is going to take some time. I am sorry to tell you that your career will not change five minutes after you finish reading this book. There are a few areas where you will be able to apply what you have learned immediately, and yes, you will see some fantastic and measurable improvements. However, the overall impact, the full benefits of this book will take some time to develop.

With that, at the end of each semester, I mean chapter, you will find a Semester Review. You may find Semester Assignments at the conclusion of some chapters as well. This is serious and you need to take it seriously.

I also highly recommend that you get a piece of paper or something and title it, "Learning Assignments" or, "Things I need to learn." As you go through this book, you will find dozens of business applications, research topics and areas of study that you need to know. You need to start a list and write these things down as you read. Take this seriously.

While those who take this very seriously will find their development time may only be a few weeks or months, for others it could be years before the full breadth of this book begins to come to fruition and you gain all of the necessary knowledge to earn a PhD. All of this will depend on the diligence with which you apply the new knowledge and principles.

Now, with that disclaimer firmly in place, let's go to work, or should I say to school!

CHAPTER 1

Selling is a Profession

Is The Doctor In?

First, please understand this: selling is a profession. Let me say that again:

SELLING IS A PROFESSION

This is the first area where you must change your thinking. You have to change your perception of who you are and what you do. You must raise the level of your own image as well as that of your job.

Think about this: If you were to go to your friend, relative or practically anyone who has never been in sales, and

John R. Landrine

ask them to name five *professional* people, what would they say?

If you were to ask almost anyone to name five *professions*, what would they tell you? Be honest. Better yet, just try it for yourself.

More likely than not, they would list many positions that they consider to be professional and they would include occupations such as attorneys, doctors, nurses, people in computers and information technology, accountants, and so forth. However, how many people would list the local used car salesperson as a professional?

How many people would add the jewelry store clerk, the door-to-door vacuum cleaner sales rep or the last telemarketer who called them to the list of professionals? People will even name their contractor, the handyman, the gardener and the plumber before they list the insurance agent. Sadly, you can even ask most *sales people* to list professionals and most will not even list themselves!

Professional selling is as much a reputable profession as any other profession and a professional sales person is as much a professional as any other professional.

Selling is a profession, but it has lost much of the respect and admiration of society due to an all-too-often lack

8

of professional service, quality products and an all-around unprofessional representation of the field by many undertrained, inadequate and apathetic people who *call* themselves sales professionals.

Before we even get into the 5 B.A.S.I.C. Steps and courses to earning a PhD, you first have to realize the incredible value and importance of who you are and what you do. As a qualified sales person, not only is your job a profession, but it is the most important profession in the entire world!

The Most Important Profession in the World

Yes, I believe that we as professional sales people have the most important profession in the whole world, and I do not make that statement lightly. Consider the following generic example and substitute what you do in the appropriate places.

Let's take a hypothetical sales person, I'll call her Susan, who sells photocopier and printer systems. After prospecting and making an appointment and a successful sales interaction, Susan closes a sale to a small company called ABC Accounting. Susan supervises the order, the delivery and the setup, conducts some training and she has a satisfied customer.

While it may appear that Susan only helped and interacted with her customer, actually she helped and touched the lives of hundreds, perhaps thousands of people.

First, Susan's company is also the manufacturer of the copiers and they have a small plant that employs 54 people. If Susan and other sales people do not sell copiers and close sales, what happens to all of those people at the plant? The only reason the plant is able to operate, the only reason that the plant is open, the only reason those 54 people have jobs is because Susan sells copiers.

However, although her company manufactures the copiers, they do not make every component of the copiers. Susan's company, like most, purchases the integral parts that make up the copier from various companies around the country and the world.

They buy the electrical components from four different companies, two of which are in Asia. They buy the moving gears from another company and the printing parts from yet another. The light bulbs and photoelectric parts come from a large firm on the other side of the country and they get the ink from another company.

For mathematics sake, let us assume that each of her company's thirty-two suppliers has 20 employees. That's another 640 people who are out of work if Susan does not sell copiers.

Now, I know that some may be thinking that it is not that simple and that there are many other factors involved, and, yes, there are. However, in *essence*, at the very core, this is exactly what is happening. So bear with me as I continue to explain the point.

Let's take this a step further and consider the numerous shipping companies that are involved in transporting these parts all over the world. Then, think of the companies that each supplier uses; they each have their own suppliers as well.

If Susan does not sell copiers, her company cannot buy lights from the light bulb company, who cannot buy glass from the glass place, who cannot buy chips from the mineral company in Silicon Valley, who can no longer use the shipping company...and so on.

Finally, if all of these people are out of work, then what happens to the local businesses they all support, like the local supermarkets, the movie theaters, restaurants, and department stores? If Susan does not sell copiers, the local economy will fall apart.

Then, if the economy of these local communities fell apart, what would happen to the economy of each respective state? If the states are suffering, then what happens to the overall economic condition of the United States?

If the economy of the United States is in shambles, then we know that it adversely affects the state of the entire world.

Susan, by selling a copier, is in part responsible for the successful operation of the whole world. Susan has the most important job on earth!

Exaggeration or Fact?

Now many people are thinking that the above example is a ridiculous, if not gross exaggeration of the truth. However, the essence of the example is true.

The fact is that:

Nothing in the world happens until a sales person sells something.

It is a fact that *a sale* of some sort, is at the heart of everything that happens in the whole world. Think about that.

You might think that when you bought that last video, there was no sales person who sold it to you. You just decided that you wanted it and went and bought it.

You may think that when you decided to purchase a new flat screen television, no sales person had anything to do with it. You did your research online and decided what you wanted to buy. You then went to a website and ordered the TV. There simply was no sales person involved.

Not true.

You may think that you decided to get up, go out and buy that video, but how did you first hear about that video? Did you see a preview of the video? That preview was an elaborate sales presentation that a sales professional put together.

You did your research and then all you did was go to the website and order that TV. However, how did you do that research? Most of the information you researched was compiled and designed by professional sales and marketing people.

Then you made your decision and went to a website designed by sales and marketing professionals and digital sales pros helped you find the website in the first place. Though sales people may not have done the actual constructing of the site, you can bet that marketing professionals controlled the design, flow and the aesthetics of the site.

You make all of the decisions, buy everything online and ship it all by Amazon. That's great. You chose Amazon and you never saw a sales person, right?

At the time of this writing, Amazon's annual marketing budget was somewhere between $850 million and one billion dollars. That, of course, was only for marketing in the United States, not the rest of the world.

Amazon is selling to you constantly and it is the most sophisticated kind of selling, that in which you never realize that they were selling to you.

Nothing happens until a sales person makes a sale. Sales people are responsible for almost everything that happens in the world, both good and bad.

So, do I believe that the latest economic crash and recent recessions are because of sales people?

Yes!

The housing market takes a nosedive as buyers complain that they are not be able to afford the high prices.

Nothing in the world happens until a sales person sells something.

However, "I can't afford it..." is an objection! Should more sales people have been able to overcome that objection, then more homes would have sold. If sales people helped homeowners sell more homes, then as those housing prices began to slowly decline and get more into balance, the economy would have stabilized.

What about high unemployment? Yes, you can blame sales people. When businesses do not do enough business, when they do not have enough customers, businesses have to cut costs. Unfortunately, employees are usually at the top of most employers' hit lists when it comes to shaving expenses.

Should those businesses have had more business, if the restaurant had more patrons, the auto dealer sold more cars and the store sold more flat screen TVs, they wouldn't have to let people go.

Remember the example of Susan and copier sales. When Susan fails to sell enough copiers, people lose jobs, period.

My point is that you must understand that selling is a profession and it is the most important and noble profession in the free world. You must understand that when you make a sale it affects more than just your pocketbook. What you do has far-reaching implications and involves more people and lives than you can imagine.

Who is the most important person in your company? Is the founder or owner of your firm the most important person in the company? How about the CEO?

Understand that if you do not make sales, no one in your company has a job. No one.

Understand who you are.

Understand what you do.

Understand the critical responsibility you have to the health and welfare of thousands of people.

Are All Sales People Professionals?

Selling is a profession and it is the most important and noble profession in the world. The question then arises; is every sales person a professional? The answer is "No."

Not everyone who calls him or herself a sales person is a sales professional. In fact, if that were the case, the sales profession would have a much better overall image and reputation in the eyes the public and there would be no need for this book.

So then, how do you know if you are a true professional? What is it that makes someone a professional? That is a good question.

Let's look at a few dictionary definitions of the word "profession" and see what it actually means to be a professional.

pro·fes·sion

- A paid occupation, especially one that involves prolonged training and a formal qualification

- An occupation (as medicine, law, or teaching) that is not mechanical or agricultural and that requires special education

- A paid occupation, especially one that involves prolonged training and a formal qualification

Merriam-Webster

: a type of job that requires special education, training, or skill

: a calling requiring specialized knowledge and often long and intensive academic preparation

As you can see, there are two common denominators in every definition of the word profession:

Prolonged training and specialized education

So, you are a professional **IF** you have had prolonged training and specialized education in the field for which you practice.

With that, ask yourself, are *you* a professional? Have you had *prolonged* training in your field? I'm afraid the two or three hours of product training you received when you joined the company does not qualify as prolonged training or specialized education, nor does reading a couple of books on sales techniques.

Are You A Professional?

I said earlier that,

Professional selling is as much a reputable profession as any other profession and a professional sales person is as much a professional as any other professional.

Now allow me to qualify that statement. Please note I say that professional selling is as much a profession as any other profession. So, let us look at another profession and see what makes *them* a professional. Let us see just what it means to acquire prolonged training and specialized knowledge.

Let's take a look at a medical doctor. Most everyone would consider a doctor of medicine to be a professional, right?

Look at an average medical doctor who after high school, goes on to study for 4 years to complete a bachelor's degree. The student then

> You are a professional *IF* you have prolonged training and specialized education in the field for which you practice.

goes to medical school for 4 years and then to a residency (on-the-job training), for an average of 4 years. Finally, if the doctor is to specialize in certain types of medicine, he or she commits to another 2 to as many as 7 years in *fellowship*.

So, after 12 years of grade-school, the average medical doctor invests another 12 years of school, education and training before they ever go to work!

On average in the United States, a medical doctor spends 50,000 to 60,000 hours of study and training before going into practice.

The average medical doctor in the U.S. spends 50,000 to 60,000 hours of study and training before going into practice.

However, that's not all. Let's add another average of 25 hours every year in CMEs (Continuing Medical Education or CEUs, Continuing Education Units) that are mandatory to keep his or her license to practice medicine.

That is a professional.

Now compare yourself to that. Seriously. Can you point to 50,000 hours of time invested in studying and learning the practice of selling?

How about 5,000 hours? That's all, just 10%. Most sales people cannot find as many as 5,000 hours of training and study that they have invested into their profession. Is it any wonder why that surgeon makes $250,000 a year and the sales rep makes $25,000?

Can I get brutality honest? Most sales people could not point to even 500 hours of true, tangible professional education and training. Can you find 500 hours of sales education over your entire career? If you cannot, can you really complain that you do not make enough money?

Aw. That hurt your feelings, huh? Good. But don't feel too bad because it is the norm. However, selling is more than just working hard and putting in hours. You have to know what you are doing.

Now, you do not have to compare yourself head to head with such a *technically* demanding field as medicine. In fact, for most selling occupations, you'd be hard pressed to even *find* 50,000 hours of anything to study.

So, let's use a figure for the average professional of just 8,000 to 10,000 hours of baseline, core, foundational training, plus 4 years OJT (on-the-job-training, apprenticeship or residency), followed by an undemanding continuing education of only 24 hours a year.

Therefore, a sales professional should have:

A. 8,000 to 10,000 hours of baseline foundational training and education

B. 4 years OJT or residency

C. A minimum of 24 hours a year of continuing education

With those minimal standards of a professional, how do you measure up?

How much time, study and training have you invested in your career? Be honest.

- ✓ How many hours have you invested in reading?
- ✓ How many hours have you spent in reading about your industry?
- ✓ How many hours of study have you invested in researching the history and future of your product?
- ✓ How many hours have you spent in reading and researching the laws and regulations of your industry?
- ✓ How many hours have you spent in sales training?
- ✓ How many sales books have you read?
- ✓ How many sales training courses have taken?

✓ How many seminars have you attended?

✓ How many industry conferences have you attended?

While the average sales person may have a college degree, rarely does that degree or area of study align with or have anything to do with what they sell or even with the sales profession.

The average sales person in the U.S. receives 5 to 10 hours of product-specific training. Most sales people also accumulate roughly 15 to 20 hours of sales training or study in the form of books, CDs, or seminars of some sort, for a total of about 25 to 30 hours, plus a scarce 1 to 2 hours of continuing education per year. The average sales person also receives about 10 hours of product specific training for each company or product that he or she sells.

Therefore, when we total this all up, we see that in America and the UK, an average sales person who has been in the field of sales for 10 or 15 years can easily have *less* than 100 hours of actual prolonged study and specialized education in the field of selling.

100 hours vs. 50,000 hours

According to Study.com and the U.S. Bureau of Labor Statistics, to become a professional plumber in the United States takes an average of 4 to 5 years of classroom style training and education combined with 1,700 to 2,000 hours of on-the-job training or apprenticeship, *before* you can qualify to take the exam to become a licensed professional plumber. That's easily 3,000 to 4,000 hours before you are allowed to even take the test to get a professional plumber's license in most states.

Can you honestly call yourself a professional if you are sitting on a grand total of 35 or 52 hours of training and professional education? That, my friends, does not a sales professional make.

So just how do you get to 8,000 hours of study and 24 hours of continuing education? Where do you find that much to study? Stay tuned and I will soon show you exactly how and where to get the education you need to earn a PhD.

Invest in Your Profession

In addition to the incredible amounts of time a medical doctor puts into his or her career, the average doctor also invests $166,750 into the effort. So, as I begin to tell you that you need to buy a few books, take in a couple of trade shows and spend a little money here and there, you really should not get upset.

At the beginning of your career, or as soon as possible, you should get those 10 hours of training and information from the company you work with. However, do not stop there. Aggressively pursue *all* of the information that you can get from your firm. Realize, though, that your company information and training material is biased.

Therefore, also seek out every bit of information on every competitive company that you can find, and everything that you can find on your industry. In short, you need to look up and study everything there is to look up and study about what you do. Read *everything*.

Then you need to read, study, listen to, participate in or watch as much sales training material as you can. Some of the information will be extremely valuable, while some may not only be useless, it may even be a bit harmful. But that's okay. You need information. You will prove for yourself what works and what does not work over time. In the interim, just take in everything that you can.

So you're ready to start selling life and health insurance. You've passed your life and health licences for your state and got your 6/63; congratulations. That process gave you some great foundational study hours to start. But what have you done since?

Okay, you had to go to a couple of seminars, but how much more have you done on your own? How much more have you studied? Do you think that you now know all there is to know about life or health insurance? What do you read daily? Do you subscribe to industry magazines? Which ones?

You should consume at least four books or the equivalent of such, every month. That is, read, listen to, watch or participate in at least four books every month. Early in my career, I used to take in an average of eight books every month.

If you read a lot of articles and blog posts, consider the average article is about 300 words, so about 100 articles equals one book. Your book intake should include a mixture of technical material

> **You should consume at least 4 books or the equivalent every month**

such as those related to enhancing your industry and product knowledge and skills and techniques. Then balance that out with subject matter that is inspirational, motivational and uplifting. You need have a steady diet of both.

You do not want to have a ton of material that pumps you up, yet gives you no skills to close a sale. Conversely, it is not good to have a plethora of knowledge if you are going to cave in and give up as soon as you have a bad week.

Go ahead and credit yourself with 20 hours for every book that you absorb and one-half hour per article. If you complete your four books every month, and your company provided training, then in just 1 year, you will have about 970 hours invested.

Now, if you read only two books a month, then it could take you 2 years to get to 970 hours. If you read one book a month, then it could take you 3 or 4 years. Do you see why this is up to you?

In addition, we will make a stipulation for all of the books you have read and the studying you have already done to this point. Just like any good university program, you will get credit for past course study as well as life experiences similar to CLEP, DSST or ECE credits.

After your eight books a month and 10 hours of company training, you should then participate in at least one seminar, training course or otherwise in-depth classroom-style program every 3 or 4 months. When you factor in after-class study and practice, each such a course should provide you with about 25 hours for another 100 hours a year.

Finally, you need to have some type of residency or apprenticeship too, just like a doctor, a plumber or any other professional. Let's face it, you are not going to begin your career as a seasoned sales person, any more than someone starts out as a seasoned dentist or attorney. You have to start somewhere. You have to gain some practical field experience.

You have to have a period of OJT (On-the-Job Training), internship, apprenticeship or residency.

You should go through the equivalent of a 4-year residency/internship program or on-the-job training period. You can consider the first 4 to 8 years of your career as that on-the-job training.

You should have a 4-year residency/internship or on-the-job training period

However, in sales, it is not about *time*. Selling is about *experience*. Selling is much like an automobile; it's not the age, it's the mileage that counts.

As an example, let's consider two sales people who both work for ABC Widgets. We have sales person Mary and sales person Bob. They both start with the company on the same day and both have no prior sales experience. At the end of 1 year, who would you say has the most sales experience?

A. They both have the same amount of sales experience
B. Mary has more experience
C. Bob has more experience
D. It depends on who saw the most prospects and customers and who did the most presentations.

Selling is about experiences, not time. You measure experience in sales by how many people you talk to, how many telephone calls you make and how many sales interactions you have had. These sales related activities are called "sales metrics." Some also call these sales activities, KPIs – Key Performance Indicators. While there is a difference between sales metrics and KPIs in that every sales metric is not a *key* metric or key indicator of performance, for most sales processes we will use the broader term of sales metrics.

These sales metrics are the only way that you can measure your actual performance to get a true representation of your real experience.

Let's say that over that first year of employment with ABC Widgets, Bob stayed close to his quota and met with and attempted close 50 prospective customers.

However, during that same year, Mary worked much harder, made more telephone calls and had more appointments. As a result, she met with and attempted to close 100 prospects.

Although they both worked with the same company for the same calendar year, Mary actually has more sales experience than Bob. Does that make sense?

With the example of the medical doctor, let us take two heart transplant surgeons who both have been practicing for

10 years. Over that time, one doctor has performed 15 heart transplants and the other performed 200 heart transplants. Can we reasonable say that both doctors have the same amount of experience?

So when I say that you need to have 4 years of sales experience or apprenticeship as the foundation for your career, what does that mean? Four years as a sales person, *in time only*, means nothing.

You have to have a method to equate time with real sales experiences. You must use sales metrics instead of sales hours to understand your actual experience. There is a big difference between *calendar* time and *sales* time. You have to discern the difference between a calendar year and what I call a "Sales-Metric Year."

The Sales-Metric Year

You have to be able to separate actual sales time and performance from regular time. Here is a method to convert a calendar year into a *sales metric year*.

First, take the amount of sales it takes in 1 year to be the top sales person in your company. How many sales does the #1 sales person sell or close in 1 calendar year?

Then take the company's overall closing average. That is, find out from your sales management what the company's general closing average is for all sales people. You do not want the closing average of the *top* person, but for the *average* sales person.

You want to figure out how many sales presentations or closing attempts, it takes the average sales person to make *one* sale.

Once you have a closing average, then calculate how many sales presentations or closing attempts it would take to sell the amount of sales the top person sold in 1 year.

How many sales presentations would the *average* sales person have to make to be the top sales person in the company? This amount of presentations or closing attempts is your *Sales Metric Year*.

Here's an example:

Top sales person's number of closed sales in one year is

100

The company's overall closing average is

20%

(Or 1 out of 5)

Number of presentations it takes to close those 100 sales with a 20% closing average is

500

In this example, when you complete
500 closing attempts,
you would have completed one sales metric year.

So how long would it take you to complete 500 closing attempts? If you made 2 closing attempts a day, 5 days a week for 50 weeks, at the end of exactly one calendar year, you would have 500 closing attempts. In this case, your calendar year would be equal to a sales metric year.

However, let's say that you only averaged 1 closing attempt per day, 5 days a week for 50 weeks; then at the end of a full year, you would only have 250 closing attempts which is really the equivalent of only 6 months true sales experience. Does that make sense?

Then, on the other hand, if you completed 3 closes a day, 5 days a week, you would reach a year's worth of sales experience in less than 8 months. In a calendar year, you would have 1 ½ *sales metric years* of experience.

I hope this is making sense to you, especially if you are rather new to selling or new to these concepts. It is important that you get a firm grasp on where you are right now, where you *really* are right now.

The main problem is if you get bogged down in the time and how many years you've worked here or there, it is too easy to fool yourself into believing that you have more actual sales experience then you do.

Look back over your career and figure this out. Of course, you will be guessing at some of these numbers, but just be honest.

You know what your performance was like at that company you worked with 10 years ago. You know what you did. You may not have the exact numbers, but you know how you performed.

You know that the company called for 5 presentations a day, but you were young and wild and took off early at least twice a week to join your friends for happy hour or to see a movie with your girlfriends. Be honest.

As we start to get into this and the truth of your performance and work ethic starts to become clear, you will likely begin to increase your efforts, but be realistic about the past. If you do not have much of a past to speak of, then keep track and be honest as you go.

A Calendar Year =
X amount of months

A Sales Metric Year =
X amount of sales metrics
(Or specific KPIs such as closing attempts)

It has to be about the amount of people you have seen, talked to and tried to close. It also has to take into consideration and reward extra effort and performance. After all, selling is a performance-based business.

****************** STOP*****************

If you are still not certain on exactly how to figure out your Sales Metric Year or if the preceding information is not clear to you, then I urge you to stop, go back and re-read this section. If you are sure you got it...then let's move on.

****

So, you need 4 sales metric years OJT or apprenticeship, residency. How long will that take in real time? It depends on you.

Adding it All Up

I am saying that before you can even to begin to be a true professional you need 8,000 to 10,000 hours of prolonged study and education, plus 4 years OJT/residency (of true sales experience not time) followed by 24 hours a year of continuing education. So let's begin to add up these experiences using a hypothetical sales person with the numbers below.

Total Hours

Let's take a look at Johnny Gogetter who has been with ABC Widgets for one full calendar year and see what has happened. After one calendar year, Johnny has...

✓ Received 10 hours of company provided training

✓ Consumed 4 books every month,

✓ Has had 12 months of calendar time in the field

Adding it up:

- The 10 hours of company training = 10 hours
- 48 books (20 hrs. per book) = 960 hours
- 12 calendar months, but according to his sales metrics, he has 15 months OJT.

Total investment time in one calendar year:

970 hours of study and 15 months

At this rate, he will get the 4 years OJT fairly quickly, but it may take him 8 years of study, or should I say

of prolonged training and specialized education

You might think, "8 years of study! Gosh, that sounds like studying to get a PhD." Exactly!

What could he do to get there faster? Well, he could find and insist on more company training and material, go to 1 seminar or conference every quarter and invest in 1 training seminar (CDs, DVDs, online, etc.) a month and it would look like this:

- 30 hours of company training = 30 hours
- 48 books (20 hrs. per book) = 960 hours
- 4 seminars/conferences (x 25 hours) = 100 hours
- 12 CD seminars (x 25 hours) = 300 hours
- 1 Sales Metric Year Residency

Now you have 1,360 hours a year, which would now take him a little under 6 years to earn a PhD.

Also, remember that your 4 years residency runs concurrently. So in that last example you could earn a doctorate in sales in just under 6 years. That's not bad. Not bad at all.

Homework

So, here is your first assignment: Sit down and calculate how much time, sales time that is, you have invested in your career thus far. It does not matter if you have been in the business for 15 years or 15 days. When you sit down and look at your experiences from this perceptive, you may find that you have a lot less experience than you may have once thought.

Yes, this will take a little time and some effort, but this is important to know. Even if you have been around the world of selling for many years, you still want to see how much time you have been investing every year.

This will also let you see just how serious you have been about your career thus far. If looking back you see that for most of the years you have been in the business you have lingered around 75% of par, it will tell you something. You may look back and find that for most of your career you have been skating and getting by on the minimal amount of work. That's a wakeup call, Doc! (and I use the term lightly)

Go back in your mind, back to that first sales job you had, and remember the best you can, what happened there.

How much time do you actually invest today? If you have only been in sales for three, four or five years, then this exercise alone will position you to leap years ahead of your peers.

If you struggle to remember the books you've read or classes you have taken, estimate it the best you can. Just be honest with yourself.

You will find an overview of what you need to do in the Semester Assignments.

Semester Review

CHAPTER 1

Selling is a Profession

---

1. Selling is a profession just as much as is the profession of law, medicine or accounting. Selling is the most important profession in the world. However, not all sales people are professionals.

2. You are responsible for the well-being of tens of thousands of people. No matter what you sell, when you make sales, you help thousands of people all around the world.

3. Becoming a true sales professional requires years of prolonged training and specialized education. It does not happen overnight and there are no shortcuts.

4. You need to acquire 8,000 to 10,000 hours of foundational training and specialized education, 4 years OJT or residency, followed by a minimum of 24 hours per year in CE (Continuing Education) to become, and maintain the status of a sales professional.

5. You need to read or consume at least four books per month: two on technical skills-based teaching and advice, and two on motivation, inspiration and mental conditioning type subject matter.

6. You need to attend at least one industry seminar, tradeshow or conference every quarter.

Semester Assignments

1. **Company Training** - Figure out how much training time (in hours) you have received from your company (or companies) in the form of classes, seminars, sales training, sales training-based meetings and digital or written material. Add 20 hours for book-length written material and fractions thereof for smaller documents.

2. **Outside Training** – Figure out how much time you have invested in training other than that provided by companies that you have worked with.

3. **Additional Training and Study** – Add in all the additional time invested on any sales training or self-improvement/motivational study you have done since the beginning of your career.

4. **Sales Time** - Now calculate and add in the time you have spent in the field actively selling, particularly in the first 4 or 8 years of your sales career. Calculate your accumulated sales metrics and calculate your sales metric years from the beginning.

5. **Continuing Education** – Finally, calculate how much time in books and everything else you commit to your sales career on an ongoing basis per month or year. Please note that time in the field, OJT does not count toward this type of training time. Here you need books, seminars, etc.

Calculate how much time you have accumulated and how much more you need to get to 8,000+ hours of foundational training. If you have surpassed 8,000 hours, congratulations, but don't stop there.

Also, add up how many hours in CEs you get every year. If the amount is less than 24 hours a year, figure out now how you can increase that time.

Remember also that some things, like reading books, do not stop...ever. You don't necessarily have to continue at the pace of 4 books a month, but you need to read at least one a or two a month. Then of course, you may already know that as you are reading this book!

You may be thinking, "My gosh, that's going to take an awful amount of work and time!"

Yes, yes it is.

Oh, I might add that the time it takes you to compete this assignment...counts!

CHAPTER 2

The B.A.S.I.C.s

I have been very fortunate and blessed to have such a wonderful sales career. From selling candy door-to-door at 9 years old, to closing sales with county governments and Fortune 500 firms, to managing and training hundreds of sales people over the course of more than 35 years, it has been a blessing, to be able to be a blessing to so many people.

During that time, I have trained thousands of sales people, some directly and many through articles, books and digital media. I have also seen hundreds of tricks, gimmicks and fads come and go, all of which promised to transform the sales careers of the average or mediocre sales person with the wave of some magical wand.

While I have no doubt that these magical scripts and supernatural tips get their share of attention and make the authors rich, they are usually based on pep-rally rah, rah, sis boom bah, rhetoric or the theoretical assumptions of arm-chair executives who have little or no first-hand sales success experience.

These books and audio seminars cause an initial spark of excitement, yet eventually leave the sales person in the same or worse position then which they began.

Such material, based on instant gratification and glorification, has ended the sales careers of countless would-be-one-day sales heroes and quenched the dreams of more than a few families.

A successful sales career does not come from opening up a can of a *get-rich-quick and crackers*. However, over the years, I have found that there are a few foundational principles that not only make successful sales careers, but seem to be what has made the difference between a successful career and an *exceptional* career.

There are thousands of sales people, true professionals, who manage to have wonderfully successful careers, earning lots of money, solving problems for tons of people, winning all kinds of awards and making a mark on the world.

However, a select few sales people somehow manage to rise above everyone else. Some people seem to become more than *just* sales people. Some people appear literally to have selling and professionalism running as blood through their veins. They never lose a sales contest, never miss a sales award and their integrity is never in question. I'm talking about those sales people who seem to elevate the position of a sales professional to another level.

There are some people whose minimum performance metrics, dwarf the top performance of the average sales person.

These are the record breakers and holders. These are the leaders that most sales people feel they learn something from just by being in their presence.

Do you know the type of sales person I am talking about? Have you met one?

These professionals have earned a PhD in the Sales.

Earning My PhD

I remember when I believe I had earned my PhD in professional selling. Although I was just a young 28 years old, I had already amassed far more than 10,000 hours in training and specialized education. In fact, it was probably closer to 50 or 60,000 hours at that time. Plus, I was getting easily 75 to 100 hours a year in CEs every year since I was appointed to my first sales management position at the age of 21. I also had the time invested. However, it was during one week when I was a Regional Sales Manager at Gulf Industries Corporation (now Signtronix) that made me realize where I truly was in the world of selling.

It was one of those weeks that I had designated as a *"Beat the Boss Week."*

As the regional manager, I had less than half the available time as my sales team had to actually get out in the field and close my own sales. However, I still managed to keep up with my sales crew in personal sales, and was often the top sales person. I truly believe in leading by example.

Well, every once in a while, maybe 3 or 4 times a year, I would take one week off from managing, get out there in the trenches, and go head-to-head with my sales team. I often did this at times when sales where slow and a negative atmosphere was trying to take hold.

I had a *Beat the Boss Week* at times when sales team members began to believe in the economy objection they were hearing from prospects, or when they began to believe that the area had become over saturated and buyer-poor, or when some other pessimistic, stinkin' thinkin' began to permeate the minds of my sales people.

Beat the Boss Week would completely reenergize my sales crew and laser target any cancerous thinking and utterly destroy it. The sales crew lived for *Beat the Boss Week.*

Beat the Boss Week also carried some huge monetary prizes and awards. The main prize went to the sales person who managed to outsell me during that week. I rewarded that sales rep with a prize that was easily the equivalent of a more than a month's pay. However, the fringe benefits became the most sought after prize of the contest. That sales person would hold the most coveted position and badge of honor of having gone head-to-head with me and won.

Did it ever happen? Did any of my sales people ever take me on head-to-head and win? I'll share that later in the book. For right now let's go over getting your PhD.

The B.A.S.I.C.s of a PhD

Over the years, I have found a few foundational ideas and standards that have proven to be the common denominator of leading sales people to extraordinary heights in sales and of leading sales professionals to the degree of Doctorate of Sales. It is on these foundational principles and best practices that I formed the BASICs.

I actually formed the basis of the BASICs over 15 years ago and had written and published the concept in short articles and blogs around the world. However, it is only now that I decided to expound on the concept to help sales people get over the new hump they find in facing today's new and sophisticated consumers.

If you have been selling for any significant amount of time, then you have probably found that most of the techniques that you have learned do not actually work. You have found that most of those so-called golden-nuggets that your sales manager gave you also do not do well in the real world.

The problem with most of today's sales training and techniques is not that they actually do not work. The problem is that sales people are using them on the wrong prospects. The prospective buyers for which most of today's sales techniques were originally created, simply no longer exist. That prospect does not exist. That customer is not here anymore.

Today's Consumer Has Changed

The fact is that today's consumer has changed. The average prospective customer that sales people approach today is nothing like those of just 10 or 15 years ago. They may even be the same people, but they are not of the same mindset.

In the past, the customer had to depend largely on the *word* of the sales person for almost everything. If the sales person said that his product had the best rating in the industry, the buyer could not quickly verify the information one way or the other. The price that the sales person quoted was THE price...period. If the sales person said that she had no complaints against her or her company, then that customer had to either accept her word or not.

Much of successful selling in the past involved the prospect's personal belief in the sales person. Much of the prospects' buying decision hinged on whether the customer could *believe* and *trust* what the sales person said.

Therefore, the sales training philosophy of the time revolved around helping the prospect feel more confident in the sales person. The primary objective was to get the customer to have confidence in and believe in the sales person and the sales company. Sales techniques taught sales people ways to demonstrate knowledge so the customer would believe that the sales rep was an industry authority and consequently, believe what he or she said. The primary focus of sales techniques was to build up the credibility of the sales person, with the secondary objective being to raise the value and credibility of the product or service.

This is where the idea of "selling yourself first" came from. I never believed in the *sell yourself first* ideology, but I understand the logic behind it and why so many people adopted such a practice. The thought was that if you could first get the prospect to buy into *you*, to like you and trust you; then the odds where good that they would buy your product.

Of course, that is not factually accurate; however, there was a small element of truth to that concept.

Selling was about leveraging information that the customer did not have and therefore had to rely on the sales person. The bottom line is that in the past, sales techniques largely capitalized on the *ignorance* of the customer.

Since 15 or 20 years ago, the prospect did not have much else to go on but what the sales person said, then it did make some sense first to get the prospect to like you. That was then. However, that is far from the situation and climate in which we operate today.

> **Sales techniques in the past capitalized on the ignorance of the consumer**

Today, the average consumer is more educated, sophisticated and sales savvy than ever before. Today's consumer also has an entire world of information instantly available, literally at their fingertips in the form of the internet.

Gone are the days when the prospect had to rely on what the sales person said. In this new millennium, the customer can and often does have more information about your products, services, service records, industry standing, reputation and prices than you may have. The customer can also already have a complete dossier on you before you even show up.

By the time you arrive for the appointment or when the customer comes into your place of business, often that buyer already knows the price ranges of what you sell, the guarantees and warranties, available discounts and everything else they need to know. Today's consumer no longer has to rely on what you say and some don't really care about what you say.

In addition, most customers today are in some way, sales people themselves. Practically every sales manager, business owner or supervisor is involved with a company that sells *something*, and each does what he or she can do to gain every advantage in their marketplace. Many of the customers you call on today have read some of the same sales books and taken some of the same sales training courses that you have had. Is it any wonder why some of those old tried and true classic sales closes no longer work?

Finally, add in the fact that competition today is as fierce as it has ever been, everything moves at the speed of light, businesses have become more cutthroat and customers less loyal; and you are looking at a completely different sales environment and prospective customer. That same old *Ben Franklin Close* that worked so well just few years ago is a dinosaur fossil today.

Today's tactics must take into account that the consumer is smarter and more aware. The modern sales approach must be one that is more inclusive of the prospect's understanding and must attempt to capitalize more on knowledge rather than ignorance.

Successful sales understanding must be rooted in absolute truth and genuine empathy rather than slick words and manipulation. You will find the BASICs to be a true genuine,

> **Successful sales understanding must be rooted in absolute truth and genuine empathy rather than slick words and manipulation.**

empathic and consultative approach to selling.

If you want to earn a PhD in sales, then you need to acquire the sales metrics, prolonged training and specialized knowledge as listed earlier and follow these BASICs!

The B.A.S.I.C.s

The acronym BASIC stands for:

B = Believe

A = Ask

S = S.O.S.

I = I.T.

C = Care

It is actually quite simple.

1. First, you have to **B**elieve: You have to believe in what you sell and do.

2. Then you have to **Ask:** You have to know how to ask for the order with strength and conviction.

3. You have to understand **S.O.S.:** The Science Of Selling.

4. You have to understand how to use **I.T.:** information and information technology.

5. Finally, you have to **C.A.R.E.:** You have to genuinely care about your customer and about what you do.

Those are the stepping stones to the next level. Those are course requirements for the degree. If you are ready, then let's go to school!

Semester Review
CHAPTER 2
The B.A.S.I.C.s

---

1. Today's consumers have changed; they are unlike those of just 10 years ago.

2. In the past, sales techniques often relied on the ignorance of the prospect and the consumer had to rely on what the sales person said.

3. Today's consumer is more educated, sophisticated and sales savvy than ever before.

4. Many of today's consumers have had some of the same sales training as most sales people.

5. Today's sales techniques must rely on the consumers' awareness, and be based in truth, empathy and integrity.

CHAPTER 3

B = Believe

After understanding that you are a vital part of the most important profession in the world, then you have to honestly and wholehearted believe in what you do. What you truly believe about what you do, deep down in your heart, will determine how high you rise in your sales career. You must earnestly believe in not only what you sell, but also in what you do, entirely. You must believe in your mission and the results of every sale.

Many people right now are saying, "I know I believe in what I sell." However, I beg you to carefully reconsider the question. Believing in what you sell has to be a belief that stands apart from the fact that you make money when you sell it. I am referring to a different level of belief.

Very early in my career someone gave me what has proven to be the single most valuable piece of advice that I have ever received about selling.

A retiring old sales pro once told me:

"John, if you cannot heavily prospect and pursue your own mother, grandmother, wife or some other dear loved one, then sit them down and give them a full-blown sales presentation, then close hard, I mean continuing to persist, overcoming objection after objection, and then close the sale at a fair price, and then feel GOOD about the full commission you made off the sale; then do not sell that product or service because you do not truly believe in it."

Wow! Think about that. Now of course, this is assuming that your loved one is a *qualified prospect* for what you sell. If so, then yes, you should feel that way about it.

Would you feel comfortable selling what you sell to your mother, father, wife or husband? Could you look your grandmother in the face and insist that she buy what you sell and then charge her the market rate and still feel good about it?

Again, we must first assume that your loved one can qualify as a prospect for what you do and sell.

If you sell employee staffing services and your loved one does not own a business and could not possibly use your services, then it doesn't count.

However, if you sell print advertising and you have a loved one who owns a small business that could benefit from placing an ad with you, then you should want them to do business with you. Can you call on that loved one, push hard to get them to buy and close hard, persist and then feel good about earning a commission off that sale?

Perhaps you sell ladders, or scaffolding or pipes for plumbing or asphalt or something that people may not think is very exciting or sexy. You may wonder how you are supposed to be so head-over-heels in love with and believe strongly in, something so mundane.

It does not matter what the product is. The question is do you feel that your company's ladders are the absolute best in the business? Are your pipes the best on the market or provide the best overall value?

So what if you sell a product that is identical to many others on the market? You sell the exact same products as many other companies do. Okay.

Then do you believe that you and your company provide the absolute best service? Do you have the best warranties and contracts?

Do you believe the customer is better off by choosing you rather than your competition? You must believe in what you sell and what you do.

Your competitive advantage has to be more than just a slogan. It must be how you truly feel. You have to believe in what you are claiming that you and your company represent.

Sales people often ask me if it is necessary that they own the product or service that they sell. Again, if you can qualify as a legitimate prospect for what you sell, then yes, you should own that product. If you do not own what you sell, and would not sell it to people who you care deeply for, then you do not believe it what you sell.

Unfortunately, many newer or younger sales people fall into the trap of signing on with a company and selling a product purely due to the money they believe they can make.

While newer sales people often do this out of rookie ignorance rather than selfish intent, the bottom line effect is the same: A sales person whose mind is centered more on him or herself rather than the benefits to the customer.

The very first step in earning a PhD in sales is to believe wholeheartedly in what you sell and what you do.

There are tons of obvious moral and ethical reasons for this, one being that if you do not truly believe in what you sell, then you do not believe in what you are saying when you are selling.

Hence, that makes you a liar.

Actually, if you do not believe in what you tell others to believe in, you are not even a sales person; you are a con-man or con-woman. In fact, that is the very definition of a con artist. Con artist is short for *confidence-artist,* as in one who uses the confidence of others against them. Someone who cheats or defrauds others by gaining their confidence in something that they themselves do not believe.

However, this is not a book on morals or ethics however (though I could go on about this one topic long enough to write several books). Still, what I am talking about is more than a matter of principles or philosophical beliefs and moral standards. I am talking about business.

What I am talking about here are the many technical, tangible *business* reasons why, to be successful, you must believe in what you sell. There are many specific and practical reasons why your unbelief, your lack of personal conviction, will severely hamper your success in sales.

Four Major Business Reasons Why
You Must Be a True Believer

Here are just four reasons why you must be a true believer if you ever want to earn a PhD in sales. I'll first list them and then we will check them out one at a time.

If you **do not** truly believe in what you sell and do:

1. **You will have an inconsistent work ethic**

2. **You will discriminate against prospects and customers**

3. **There will be many objections that are impossible for you to handle**

4. **You will not be able to close with conviction**

1. You will have an inconsistent work ethic

One of the primary keys to sales success is a consistent work ethic and in this book, in the "S = S.O.S." section, you will learn some powerful ways to help you develop and maintain such a work ethic.

To rise above the average sales person, you have to develop work habits that rise above the work habits of the average sales person. You have to establish a rock-solid, rigorous, relentless working regimen in where you complete a set number of telephone calls, sales calls, presentations and other metrics every day, day in and day out, week after week, month after month.

This work ethic must be steadfast and unaffected by anything. Your work ethic cannot change from one week to the next. Your work ethic must remain consistent regardless of sales results, business ups and downs, personal problems, economic conditions or anything else.

However, when your primary motivation is the money, your work ethic will change according to your need for the money. Your work ethic will change according to your personal financial situation.

When things are pressing and your need for extra cash is high, so will be your work efforts. You will work harder. The enthusiasm, vigor and spark in your eyes, the pep in your step, will all quicken when you have a need or strong desire for more money.

However, when you are not as desperate, or the desire is not as strong, the enthusiasm and work ethic will suffer. Yes, you may feel that you always have a strong desire to earn more money.

However, you have to admit that there are times when you are more motivated for money than at other times. Your motivation fluctuates. As your motivation fluctuates, so will your work ethic. One of those times when your work ethic will fluctuate is right after you have made a big sale and a large commission.

You will try to fake it and push yourself and do all sorts of things to keep the consistency, but it will not work. The same fire will not be there when you have a bunch of money in your pocket.

Can you be a good sales person without being a true believer? Yes. However, this book is not about how to be a *good* sales person or even a great sales person. This is about how to be the top, the best of the best, how to be a sales person with a PhD in selling. If you want to rise up to the level of the very top, the very elite, then you must believe wholeheartedly.

The Root of All Evil

Please don't misunderstand what I am saying. I am not saying that money or thinking about making a lot of money is a bad thing. I am not saying that it is wrong to want to sell a product or service that will pay you very well. I am not saying that it is wrong to want to make huge commissions when you sell. I am not saying that it is a bad thing to desire financial success and rewards.

No! No. No. In fact, what I am saying is quite the opposite. I personally believe that for a *professional* sales person, a 6-figure income is just above minimum wage.

However, what I am saying is that to sell something *primarily* because of what it pays, is a short-sided view of what you do and will limit your success.

Selling something primarily because of the amount of money you will make, will severally limit the amount of money you will make.

Such a position may return some immediate financial gains, yet will not provide solid, long-term growth.

Conversely, to sell something because you truly believe in it, believe it in your heart, and which also happens to pay you well, will provide long-term wealth. It depends on how you look at what you do. How you view what you do will make all the difference.

How you see yourself, how you feel about yourself and your job will make the difference in how much money you make. This short story will help illustrate my point.

What Are You Making?

There were three men working on a construction site. They were deep down in a huge hollowed out space in the ground. It was a large square space that had been cleared and cemented over.

Each of the men was working in a different corner of this apparent soon-to-be room of some kind and each had a large stack of bricks, a bucket of cement and a trowel. They seemed to be laying bricks in each of their respective areas.

Another young man, who appeared to be a type of reporter since he carried a pencil and note pad, approached one of the men.

"Excuse me, sir," the young reporter said to the first man. "Do you mind if I ask you what you are making here?"

The worker, crouched on one knee, looked over his left shoulder, and barley missed a beat in laying the bricks as he said, "Yeah, uh, I am making $17.50 an hour."

The young journalist thanked him and went on to the second worker who was also down on one knee.

"Excuse me, sir, do you mind if I ask you what you are making here?"

The construction worker paused and rested his trowel on his knee. He turned to the reporter and replied, "Well, I am making part of a room. This space is going to be a basement area and I am making one of the corners of the room."

The reporter thanked the man very much and walked toward the third worker.

"Excuse me, sir," he asked again. "Do you mind if I ask you what you are making here?"

This bricklayer laid down his trowel. He turned and stood to his feet. He patted himself several times causing clouds of dust and plaster to monetarily engulf him and then settle to the floor. With shoulders back and chest out, he straightened himself and spoke.

"Yes sir. What I am making is the future. I am creating thousands of possibilities and opportunities. You see, this is going to be a building, but not just any building. This is going to be the tallest building in our county. You will be able to see it from miles and miles away. I hear that they are going to have to put one of those lights on the top to warn passing aircraft, it's going stand so tall!"

He took a deep breath and continued, "This is going to be the first structure of its kind in this area and there are going to be dozens of offices, businesses, stores and apartments in it.

It will be a beacon of activity and commerce and entertainment in this community. Hundreds of people will work here every day. It will provide income for hundreds of families and children.

Thousands of people will come through here every single day! This is the biggest, most important project in our community and it's all possible because of me!"

The journalist was frantically taking notes as the worker continued.

"This room is the foundation. This is the main thing that the entire building will rest on. This room, right here, supports the entire structure, and I am responsible for this corner of that foundation. Do you know that if any one of these bricks that I lay, just one, is off center or crooked, it could throw off the whole project!

This one brick that I lay, myself, I must lay as the foundation, the groundwork for what is to come. It all rests on these bricks! My bricks! It all depends on what I do and how I do it! The bricks that I lay are the most important pieces of the whole building, for without them it cannot stand. Without me, it cannot stand. I am the most important person in this entire project. Yes, I am making the future possible."

A few questions for you: (Jot down your answers in the spaces below or use a separate piece of paper)

1. Were the three construction workers all doing the same job?

2. Which one do you think would be most successful in the company and why?

3. Which would you think would be the least successful in life and why?

4. **Which one do you think would be more successful and fulfilled in life and why?**

Now some people might say that the third worker in that story just needs to decaffeinate. However, when you truly believe in what you sell, you will exude a natural enthusiasm for the product or service. Enthusiasm, loosely translated, means *the god within*, and that god, that power, will shine from you and the customer will see and feel it.

There is no substitute for that inherent excitement for your product. There are no sales techniques or answers to objections that can build more value and belief in what you sell than your natural, heartfelt enthusiasm.

Choose Wisely

So what should you do if you now currently sell a product or service that you do not really believe in?

Start looking.

Also, keep in mind that while the salary and commission rate is an issue, it may not be as much of an issue as you think.

For instance, let's say that you work with a company that pays a high salary and a 20% commission structure and it is a product that you do not truly believe in.

You will earn a lot more money working with a company that pays a lower salary and only 15% commission if you are totally head–over-heels in love with the product, because you will sell so much more. In any case, start looking for that thing that you can sell to your mom with a clear conscience.

2. You will discriminate against prospects and customers

When money is the primary goal, you will focus your time, effort and attention on customers based on how much money you think they will make you. Now, of course, in business, there is some logic to this.

That is, you have to spend more time with clients that bring in the most money, and invest less time with customers whose spending does not match your time and effort. However, all customers deserve a certain amount of attention and the highest level of professional treatment.

When you focus too much on the money, you will treat customers according to what you *think* they are worth.

While you will try not to do this, and may even think that you do not do this, it is inevitable. This way of thinking causes several serious problems.

> **When you focus too much on the money, you will treat customers according to what you *think* they are worth.**

First, your level and quality of customer service will go to the dogs. There will be accounts that you will treat as if they are nothing but a number, nothing but a dollar. Everyone has heard that sentiment before, "They just treat me like a number..." Guess where that feeling comes from?

No matter how hard you try, customers will notice how you feel about them. When you are answering questions for a *low-level* customer, your mind is thinking, "This person is wasting my time while the big payday just walked in on the other side of the lot."

You will not be able to hide your impatience, wandering eyes and fidgeting thumbs.

You have probably received this type of treatment before, yourself. Do you remember how it made you feel?

Do you remember how degraded and humiliated you felt when that sales person looked down her nose at you? Do you remember how enraged you became when that sales person treated you as if you were a bum?

When this type of thing happens, the customer's reaction goes far beyond the moment. Usually the customer is so irate that they want to retaliate.

Some people contact management, while others do everything they can to not only make sure the sales person in question does not get any credit for a sale, but they also want to make sure to buy from someone or somewhere else, and it doesn't stop there.

The poorly treated consumer usually tells *everybody* they can find about you and the poor treatment they received from your company. People will go out of their way to inform other people of the horrible service and advise them, even warn them, not to ever do business with you.

Then add the fact that today, with social media platforms like Facebook, Twitter, YouTube, Instgram and others, one irate person can wreak havoc your reputation and image. You simply cannot and will not build an extraordinary sales career that way.

Judging a Book by Its Cover

In addition, when you believe more in the money than in what you sell, you will not be able to pursue all prospective clients with the same vigor. You will literally judge books by their covers.

When prospecting, as you qualify prospective clients, you will naturally place more importance on those whom you believe will provide the larger, more lucrative accounts.

Again, while there is some business logic to this, you will often pre-judge and overdo it.

You will make *assumptions* as to what you *believe* the client can or will afford. While those assumptions may prove to be correct at times, you will be wrong far too often. When this happens, you will pursue some accounts with passion and persistence, and barely try to acquire other accounts. You will then miss more sales opportunities than you will ever realize. You will literally be stepping over dollars to pick up pennies.

When you do not truly believe in what you sell, and instead have a motivation that is based mostly on a commission, you will judge books by their covers and lose untold amounts of money.

3. There will be many objections that are impossible for you to handle

Because you do not believe in what you sell strongly enough, you do not buy or own the product or service that you sell. When you do not own what you sell, you actually create sales barriers for yourself.

You create objections that you cannot handle or negotiate when you do not own what you sell.

Again, you first have to be able to qualify as a prospect for what you sell. If you sell jet aircraft or vacation island property, or multimillion-dollar condominiums, then maybe you may not qualify as someone who could buy those things.

Or perhaps you sell enterprise software systems for large corporations and you do not run a large corporation; then you do not qualify as a prospect. No problem.

However, if you sell high-speed internet service and you live in a targeted reception area, then you should have that service yourself in your home; *and you should pay for it.* Getting the product or service free from your company is not the same. If you sell home alarm systems and you own a home, then you should own the alarm system that you sell.

Now, some people may be thinking that there are some legitimate reasons why you do not own your product.

For instance, with the alarm system example, you may say that your home was already wired with a built-in system that was there when you purchased the home. It is in perfect working condition, so there is no need to change it. After all, it makes no sense to rip out a perfectly good working alarm system and put in a new one just because you happen to work for the company.

Or you may say that the alarm system you sell is rather expensive, and although you believe in the system, it is a little more than you need at this time. You truly believe that the system you sell is the best system on the market and you are going to get yours just as soon as you can. You are a true believer in the product.

Or perhaps the situation is that you just started your job at the alarm company after being unemployed for a long time. It is naturally going to take a few months of steady income before you are financially stable enough to get one of your alarm systems.

It is not a question of whether you believe in the product or not. You do believe. It is not a question of you wanting to buy and own the product or not. It is simply that at this moment in time, for one reason or another, you cannot afford it. What is wrong with that? Where is the problem in that?

Here is what is wrong with that.

What are you going to say to the next prospect who gives you that same exact objection?

Prospect

"Well, I really like it. I mean I think it is the best alarm system on the market and I want one and I will get one. But I really can't afford it right now. You see, I was out of work for three months and I just started back. I am in the hole all over the place. It's going to take me a few months to get things back on track. But I really want that system. I'm sure you can understand that. Can you come back in a few months?"

You can use all of your rebuttals and answers to the "I can't afford it" objection, but no matter what you say, and no matter what you do, you will not be able to hide the fact that you *do understand* and agree with the prospect.

No matter what you say, in your mind you will be thinking, "Yeah, I know exactly how you feel."

No matter what, you will empathize with this prospect. In fact, the very moment that the prospect utters such a statement, it will hit you like a shotgun blast in the chest, the blood will drain from your face and you will stand there like a proverbial deer in the headlights. You may manage to say something, but remember, *the eyes don't lie.*

How about when you hear this…

Prospect

"Yes, I think it's a great system, but we just bought this house less than a year ago and it came with the system that's here now. I mean, I agree that what you have is a far better system and would make us safer. But what we have still works...granted, not as well as yours and it doesn't have all of the bells and whistles, but it works. I just can't see a need to rip this one out just yet..."

Now you may be thinking that you could never get those *exact* same objections. However, I can promise you that not only will you get those exact same objections, but you will get them all the time. You will find those objections seem to come up an inordinate amount of times as compared to other objections. The objection that you have for not buying your product or service will haunt you.

The very objections that you have for not buying what you sell, will be the same objections that prospects give you for not buying what you sell.

You will not have a *leg to stand on*, when dealing with those objections. You will empathize with the prospect, and worse, you will empathize with the objection.

If you have been in the world of selling for some time, you may want look at some of the objections that you seem to get too often. If you seem to get a particular objection over and over, it is possibly due to something that is in you.

Selling, at its core, at its very essence, is *"a transference of feeling."* If I can get you to feel about my product the same way I feel about it, then you will surely buy it. How I feel inside comes out and I transfer those feelings to the prospect. Remember that enthusiasm, it comes from within.

Therefore, if you truly believe in your heart that you cannot afford your product, then you will inadvertently and without using any words to the effect, transfer such feelings to your prospective customers. How you feel will exude from you.

I'm reminded of the quote by the famous lecturer and poet, Ralph Waldo Emerson, where he said,

"What you do speaks so loudly that I cannot hear what you say."

Certainly, what you do and how you act and who you really are deep inside, will override the words that come out of your mouth. The same holds true in the world of selling.

To Your Advantage

However, those deep-rooted feelings can work to your advantage and propel your sales career to new heights.

Take the example of the home alarm systems sales person again. This time, however, even though our sales hero feels it's a little more than he can afford at the time, he buckles down and buys the system. He finds that it was a struggle for a brief period; it hurt for a minute. But he did it and after a short time, he forgot all about the little bit of pain and extra money he invested.

However, he did find that he and his wife felt much better with the new system. Their peace of mind was at an all-time high. He found the system was simple and easy to use and they both loved the feature that allows them to operate the system from their cell phones. He loves his system.

Now, when he runs into one of those same objections:

Prospect

"Well, I really like it. I mean I think it is the best alarm system on the market and I want one and I will get one. But I really can't afford it right now. You see, I was out of work for three months and I just started back. I am in the hole all over the place. It's going to take me a few months to get things back on track. But I really want that system. I'm sure you can understand that. Can you come back in a couple of months?"

How do you think he handles this now? This sales person will speak with authority, experience and unbridled passion and enthusiasm from the bottom of his heart.

Sales Person

"Mr. Prospect, I truly understand how you feel. Believe me, I felt the same way. But I found out that the little bit of extra money is more than worth what you get in return. You will feel so much better and safer and your peace of mind will be at its highest! You and your wife will sleep so much better; it will change how you feel in the morning! You will also love this...and that...I'm telling you, my wife and I love this and that...!"

This sales person will speak from a position of strength and conviction. He will speak with truth and empathy. He won't need any scripted rebuttals or pat answers to objections!

He will transfer his true feelings to the prospect and his heartfelt enthusiasm *alone* will close the sale.

He will also never be satisfied with that objection again as he will do everything he can to HELP the prospect understand that they too *can* afford the system and that it is more than worth it.

Forgetting all the sales training and techniques in the world, there is nothing more powerful and effective than speaking right from the heart with the conviction and passion of personal experience.

Some of you may have also noticed the, "Feel, Felt, Found," technique in the above example and that is it in its truest form. *Feel, felt, found,* like everything else in sales, works best when it is the truth.

If you want a PhD in selling, you have to become your own best customer.

4. You will not be able to close with conviction

If you do not truly believe in what you sell, you will not be able to close sales or persist with confidence or conviction. If you find when you are closing, that prospective customers often get angry or upset if you continue to persist after an initial objection; then you probably do not believe in what you sell.

There is a big difference between a professional sales person and a nagging solicitor. First, we have the professional sales person who can close, and close again, and persist and persist in such a professional manner, that he or she can ask for the sale a dozen times and it seems the prospect doesn't mind.

Then there is that annoying sales person who, as soon as they ask for the order once, or the moment he or she starts to persist, it is almost as if they are badgering the customer.

The prospect feels attacked and pressured and gets angry and defensive. This person is more of an irritating peddler than a professional sales person.

Sales people and managers often ask me, what is it that makes the difference? Why is it that some sales people can ask for the sale repeatedly and the customer never gets upset, while other sales people can ask twice and the prospect is ready to call the police? Exactly what is the difference between a pesky peddler and a professional sales person?

Let me explain the difference with this illustration.

You and a dear friend or loved one are walking down the street as your friend is sharing some very exciting news with you. She is so engaged in what she is saying that she is paying no attention to where she is walking. You look up ahead and see that there is a large pothole in the street just in front of her. You try to get her attention to warn her to watch her step, but she ignores you and continues talking and walking straight ahead. You yell a little louder the second time in an attempt to wake her up, but she continues to walk toward the danger. Now you get physical, you grab her arm, and lightly shake her, but she continues heading into danger.

What would you do at this point?

A. Say to yourself, "Hey, I tried to help her but she wouldn't listen, so tough." You then give up and watch her fall in the pothole and possibly break her ankle, her neck or even worse?

B. Do whatever it takes to protect her, even if it took wrestling her to the ground, thinking, "I care about this person and I cannot stand by and watch her get hurt."

If it were someone you cared about in the least, you would do whatever you had to do to protect her from the danger. If she would not listen, you would yell, scream, and *make* her listen, even if you had to get physically violent.

Now think of closing a sale in that same context. You are talking with someone and you know that what you have is the best thing for him or her. You know and believe 100% in your heart that if you walk out of the door and you do not close the sale that this person or this person's business is going to be worse off. You believe with all your heart that this person is going to make a huge mistake that will cause harm in some way.

When you feel that way about what you sell, the customer can sense it. Remember, selling is a transference of feeling. When you truly believe that your pushing and being persistent is for the benefit of the prospect, the prospect can tell the difference.

In the example above, your friend might be a little startled or surprised at your actions, but when she looked at your face and saw the look of concern, fear and worry in your eyes, she would not fight you. Your friend would not call the police; in fact, she would thank you.

Likewise, that prospective customer will let you persist, rant, and rave all day when they feel that your motive is *unselfish*. When the prospect feels that your pressure is for their benefit and not because you just want to make a commission, they do not mind and in fact, will often thank you for your persistence.

However, when the prospect gets the slightest inkling that your persistence is because you just want to make the sale, or because you need the money, then it becomes an offense that is tantamount to armed robbery or worse. Once the prospect feels that your motive is self-centered, they become defensive and even hostile.

The difference between a professional sales person and a pesky peddler is the motive.

People used to say that I was mean when I was in the field, especially when I was at Gulf Industries. They used to say that I was horrible and used to scream and yell at prospective customers.

However, I wasn't being mean, I was just serious. And yes, I did yell some of them.

"What!? Are you listening to me!? What's wrong with you?! You got 50,000 people a day driving right past you, and they don't even know you are here!"

Yes, I yelled at them, but they knew that it came from my heart. They knew that I could care less about my commission. I believed in what I was doing so deeply, it was like I was on a mission, a crusade. Those people bought from me.

Think about it; if you are really concerned with making a sale to get your commission, you are not going to scream and holler at the customer.

One of our sales managers once said,

"None of John's customers would ever call him up to have beer; but every single one of them will call him first, when it has something to do with getting more customers into their business."

I cannot definitively explain exactly how the prospect knows what your true motive is, or if they actually realize it themselves. I'm certain the prospect is not consciously thinking, "I believe this person is just after my money..." or "This person cares about me...," at least not most of the time.

However, the prospect can and will *sense* a different level of trust. There is some truth to the old adage,

"The truth is in the eyes because the eyes don't lie."

The First Step

The first step in getting your Doctorate in Selling is to believe in what you sell. This belief, as you will soon see, will become the foundation on which you will build an unusually successful sales career.

Keep in mind also that it is a career. Your sales experience should be a lifestyle. Do not make the mistake of pursuing short-term gains. Think long-term, even if you happen to change jobs or companies. Think about your future.

If you are long into your career or nearing the conclusion of your career, understand that it is not over until it's over.

"Sales people never retire, they just close."

Semester Review
CHAPTER 3
B = Believe

1. Only sell something that you could sell to your mother or other loved one and have a clear conscience in receiving a large commission for making the sale.

2. Your unbelief will prevent you from being unusually successful because it will hamper your work ethic, force you to discriminate against certain prospective customers, prevent you from being able to handle some objections and prevent you from being able to close with conviction.

3. It is fine to desire to make lots of money, but that desire cannot be the only reason you sell what you sell. Selling something because of how much money you will make, will limit how much money you will make.

4. The difference between a pesky slick peddler and a professional sales person is what is in your heart and the consumer can tell the difference.

5. *You* must be your own best and most loyal customer.

CHAPTER 4

A = Ask

Now you have to ask. You have to ask for the order. Ask for the sale. Ask for the appointment. Ask for the money. Your first thought might be, "That's ridiculous. It's common sense to ask. I always ask." Yet, again, I ask that you carefully reexamine your thinking. One of the primary reasons for failure in this area is that sales people take this for granted.

While I am going to concentrate on only one main area where you need to ask, there are several places in the sales process where sales people fail to ask or to ask properly or with enough strength and conviction.

One of those areas is in qualifying the decision maker (DM) or qualifying the company, qualifying the prospect, especially when setting appointments on the telephone. Too often sales people spend, or should I say waste, time talking to people who are not qualified to make a decision or help move the sale forward. It is a very common situation.

The sales person is hammering away on the phone, receiving constant rejection and occasionally having the prospect hang up on him or her. Then, after facing a countless amount of faceless voices of mean, horrible people, finally a nice person gets on the line. The prospect sounds calm, cordial and open minded. She actually sounds as if she has an interest in the product, and setting an appointment with her seems assured.

Although this sales person realizes that he has not yet confirmed if this nice amiable person is the DM, now he really doesn't want to know. He does not want to ask, only to find out that this person, the only kind and accepting person he has spoken to all day, is not the DM. No! This person HAS to be the DM! Please!

So the sales person does not ask to confirm or asks in such a weak and flimsy way that he has already answered the question himself. It's that kind of asking without *really* asking. That is not asking.

However, let us only deal with asking or not asking for the sale. I am talking about the close or the closing question. How do you ask the prospect to buy? What do you say and how do you say it?

Many sales people never actually ask for the order. Instead, they expose the buying terms or conditions, and then wait for the prospect to say, "Okay...I'll take it. Where do I sign?" It usually sounds something like this:

Sales Person

"So, Bill, as I said, you will get the whole line of assessment tests for your employees, plus the certificates and the courseware and the whole thing comes to only $1,786."

Prospect

Silence

Sales Person

"And, don't forget you also get the 2-year refresher guarantee, so your staff can come back and retake any class they feel they need to."

Prospect

"Uhm, um."

Sales Person

"So, ah…that's it."

Prospect

Silence

Sales Person

"Uh…so whadda ya' think?"

This may look ridiculous on paper, but I can assure you that this is the actual close used by tens of thousands of sales people today.

Many sales people develop a tremendous fear when it comes to actually asking for the money. At that crucial moment, the sales person feels a significant amount of pressure building. The sales person gets a slight (or sometimes major) panic attack that becomes evident to the prospect. Once the prospect senses the smallest element of nervousness on the part of the sales person, it is all over.

A fearful, shaky, timid, flimsily manner of asking for the order will cost you an immeasurable amount of sales and money.

You may feel that you do not have this problem, that you do not have a shaky way in asking for the sale. But, how do you know?

How would you know if you are asking for the order with strength and conviction or not? You cannot ask yourself because you cannot judge yourself.

First, I am going to give you three major culprits that cause this timid way of asking for the order, and then we will go over them and finally explore how to avoid them. Let's hone in on earning a PhD in this stuff!

Three Major Problems in Asking for the Order

Here are the main three things that will hamper your efforts to asking for the order or asking with strength and conviction.

1. You do not believe strongly enough it what you are selling

2. You are not an expert on the product and or industry

3. You have an urgent need for the money

Those three culprits should look strangely familiar by now and I hope that you are beginning to see a pattern developing here. Let's examine each.

1. You do not believe strongly enough in what you are selling.

If you are not a true believer, you cannot feel confident that you are doing the right thing. You cannot feel certain that what you are doing, what you are asking, is best for the customer.

If you have any decency at all, then, somewhere deep down, you will feel an element of guilt. You are going to ask someone to spend money for something that you do not believe is worth the money, or any money.

You are asking someone to spend money on something on which *you* would not spend money yourself. You are asking someone to spend money on something, on which you would not ask your loved ones to spend money. Deep down you have to feel that you are ripping them off. It's hard to do that and be bold about it (for most people, anyway).

On the other hand, you might feel that it is a great product, but it is just not something that *you* would own. In that case, you are asking them to do something that you would not do. It is not a bad product, but *you* would not buy it. You feel that buying the product is beneath you, lower than you, not worthy of you. It's fine for *that* person, just not for you. This creates a type of *reverse resentment*.

You resent yourself for asking them to do that which you know you would not do.

Even if you have no adverse feelings or thoughts toward the product or service, you will develop arrogance and begin to *look down* on prospective customers.

Since they are buying something that is beneath you, then *they* have to be beneath you. This is not intentional, but such feelings are the result of such thinking.

I'll never forget, many years ago, very early in my career, when a dear friend pointed out to me that I suffered from that type of arrogance. I had that type of, "I'm better than you..." feeling toward some clients.

We were walking through Grand Central Station in New York City and I was dressed in my normal business suit and tie, when we passed a shoeshine stand.

The owner stood in front of the small booth that had two seats for customers and noticing that the shine on my shoes did not match the sharpness of my suit, the shoeshine man singled me out.

"Shine your shoes, Mister?" He boldly announced with a big smile on his face and a buffing rag in his hand. "Those shoes need to be on a par with that nice suit. It'll only take five minutes, and I'll have you on your way."

"No..." I replied, impatiently picking up my pace. "I'm good."

"I beg to differ." The shoeshine sales professional challenged. "Those shoes really need a shine."

"No thanks." I concluded as I turned my head indicating that I didn't want to discuss the matter any further.

My friend then asked, "You know he's right; you can use a shine."

"Nah…" I replied. "I do my own shoes."

"Yeah, well you can't shine your own shoes right now…" My friend insisted.

"Well, it's not that important right now." I said.

"What's the problem?" My buddy persisted.

I then made some other flimsy excuse that I cannot even remember. Finally, after a few more minutes of nagging from my friend, I said,

"Look, I don't want to do that to someone. I don't want to have someone down on their knees, shining *my* shoes. Its making them some sort of servant or something. I don't know how people sit up there like they are some kind of king while somebody shines their shoes. You have to be stuck up to do that. It's degrading to people."

I finished my impassioned explanation with the confidence that it would not only end the discussion but also enlighten my friend, whom I felt had never taken the feelings of the shoe shine person into consideration.

However, to the contrary, my buddy stopped and said, "My gosh, John! I never knew you were so stuck up!" Monetarily stunned from his reply, I stopped and just stood with my mouth wide open, ready to say what, I'm not sure.

"Yes," he continued. "You are seriously stuck up, mighty high on yourself."

"What?!" I yelled. "It's the opposite. I do the opposite. I try NOT to look down on people. I am not the one who's stuck up!"

Shaking his head, my friend explained, "The only reason you have to try not to look down on them is because deep down inside you feel that they are in a position to be looked down *on*."

"Uh! What?" I didn't understand what he was talking about and over the next few minutes my buddy helped me see the light.

He asked me if, when I hire an attorney, and pay his or her enormous fee, do I feel that I am degrading the attorney? Of course, I said no. He asked if I hired a taxi driver, would I feel that I put them down? Of course not. He went on to use several other examples including a baker, banker, a plumber and someone to cut my lawn.

He explained that the only reason I do not feel bad paying for any of those services is that I believe that they are *respectable* services. I believe that they are doing respectable work.

However, when it comes to shining shoes, deep down inside, he said that I feel it is not respectable work. I feel that shining shoes is a degrading, humiliating and demeaning thing to do.

He told me that although I can look at my plumber as someone who provides a valuable and respectable service, and I can view what my gardener does as a professional lawn service; when it comes to shining shoes, I look down my noise at them. That is why I feel so bad at accepting their services. It is my inadequacies, not theirs.

Ouch! That truly opened my eyes. He was right.

In this situation, you may feel as if you have empathy for your customers. You will feel as if you care for them, while the truth is that you pity them.

If you are not a true believer in what you sell, you will have a problem strongly asking for the money. You will feel a sense of guilt and hence a sense of distrust of yourself. You will distrust your own motives. The prospective customer will also sense this distrust, this nervousness, and then you can forget it.

If you have an issue with this, if you feel that sense of nervousness and trepidation when you begin to ask for the money, then I urge you to reevaluate your belief in what you do.

When the customer agrees to the sale, agrees to buy and to give you money, do you feel that that customer got the best end of the deal? Do you honestly feel that in a closing situation the customer is the big winner?

I will end this section with a sales close. It's a powerful close that exemplifies this point. It is called, "Close Like a Winner."

Close Like a Winner

While you will find this close to be a work of art, as it is technically sophisticated when skillfully applied; the main thing is that it is honest. This close is as powerful and as down to earth as you can get.

While it depends largely on the product or service you sell, this will work with almost anything, particularly intangibles.

The common situation for this close is where you have asked for the order a few times, but the prospect will not agree to buy and will not or cannot give you a clear objection.

In this case, you want to *help* the prospect realize that this seemingly complicated decision is actually very simple. You must be careful not to make this an attack.

You are not trying to show the prospect that it will be a mistake not to buy, but that as the buyer, they receive the most benefit.

Close Like A Winner

Sales Person

"Mr. Prospect, again I really appreciate your time here today and I have to be getting back to my office. But before I go I'd like to ask you just a couple of quick questions, if you don't mind. And please, Mr. Prospect, be as frank with me as I have been with you, OK? First, did you like what I showed you? I mean did the plan look good to you?"

Prospect:

"Oh yeah, it's great."

(The prospect should always say something like this. If not, then you know exactly where you came up short in your presentation. You have figured out the objection.)

Sales Person

"Is it clear to you how the plan (the product or service) can not only save you money, but also make a lot of money for you and your family for years, in fact for a lifetime?

(Be sure to state the immediate and long-term benefits of your product or service.)

Prospect

"Sure! I know it's a good plan."

(Again, if the answer is negative, you've found the problem.)

Sales Person

"Then let me ask you this, Bill..."

(Get a little closer and personal at this time.)

"Who do you think will get the most out of this plan; profit the most from this product, if you get it today — you and your family, me, or my company?"

Prospect

"Ah, well, I guess I would."

(A negative response and you know the problem.)

Sales Person

"Bill, then honestly, who do you think will LOSE the most if you don't get it today?"

(Do not let the person verbally answer this question or it will become an attack. I watch closely and pause briefly; just long enough for the answer to materialize mentally. Then, before the prospect can speak, I come back quickly with…)

"You see, Bill, you're not the loser here. You are the winner. You and your family are the big winner. Now let's go ahead and put this plan in force."

(I extend my right hand to shake. I will usually get the handshake and I grasp the prospect's hand firmly with both of my hands, get very close, eye-to-eye, and say,)

"Bill, I appreciate the business and you will really appreciate what we have done here today. Now let's go ahead and double check this paperwork."

(I assume the rest. Sincerity is the key: Up close, personal and sincere.)

The steps are simple:

1. Please be honest with me.

2. Did you like the product/service?

3. Can you see how it will benefit you today and tomorrow?

4. Who do you think will get the most from it if you get it today?

5. Who do you think will lose the most if you do not?

6. You are not the loser. You are the big winner.

7. Shake hands and assume the close.

Also, the tone and volume of your voice is important. Speak firmly, yet with warm empathy. Of course, this will not work in every situation, but your true belief in what you sell will help you to help more prospects.

Believe and close strong!

2. You are not an expert on the product and or industry.

The second reason that can cause you to have a weak and timid way of asking for the order is that you do not know enough about your product or the industry. Today's consumer is smart. They are very well informed and well prepared. When you run into that prospect who knows stuff, that customer who you know knows what they are talking about, you will have a timid close.

In the past, when the customer was in the dark on most things and had to rely on the sales person's word, is when sales people could speak with bold confidence. Under the conditions of the time, any sales person could speak with the assurance of an industry authority because no one could possibly challenge what he or she said.

However, today, if you don't have all of your proverbial ducks in a row, the customer will call you out on it. Essentially, it is fear that prevents you to ask for the order with strength and conviction.

In the beginning of your presentation, the prospect asked a question about a lawsuit that your company was involved in five years ago. You have no idea of what he is talking about, so you, very smoothly and quietly, sweep the issue under the rug.

A little later, the prospect asks if your company still gets the gearshift in your product from Mexico. You don't know. So, you say something that sounds like the truth, and move on.

When it comes to closing this sale, you are terrified that this prospect can see right through you. Not only is your close weak and flimsy, but you actually can't wait to get out of there. The sales person who still relies on the ignorance of the consumer is in trouble today. You have to know your stuff.

3. You have an urgent need for the money

The third major reason why you may not be able to ask for the order strongly enough is that you badly need the money. No matter how hard you try, you will not be able to hide this. You will not be able to conceal your inner feelings when the consistent thought in the back of your mind is, "I really need this sale!"

This is one of the reasons, once again, why you need to be a true believer, so that your primary motivation is not money.

The obvious question then becomes, "What if you just really and sincerely **DO** need the money?" How about when it has nothing to do with the fact that you truly believe in the product, you are just in a jam and need the money.

If your mortgage or rent is due in the next few days, and you are broke, then you really need the money, hence, you really need the sale. When your car payment is due or your lights are about to be turned off, then you need the money.

So, how do you put that out of your mind when you are closing for the sale?

That's a very good question.

You have to do two things: one, of course, is that you have to truly believe in what you sell. Then you need to put the correct value on the sale. You have to understand exactly what the sale is really worth.

The problem that arises when you are in a precarious financial situation is that you will tend to put too much emphasis on the value of the sale. Typically, as a sales person, you assign a monetary value to every sale. You mentally assign a figure to how much money you will gain from the sale.

However, this figure, this monetary value is usually out of proportion with the *true* value of the sale or the commission.

Typically, the sales person will view the value of the sale, the value and amount of the commission from closing the sale, to be well above the true value of the sale and the commission.

As a true sales professional, you have to be able to assess the actual value of the sale, and what you will gain from closing the sale, to put the sale in the proper perspective.

What I am about to briefly explain here, we will go over in more detail in the next chapter, "S = S.O.S.: The Science of Selling." However, this is a perfect segue into that enlightening chapter.

There will be times when your need for money will overshadow your belief in the product. This feeling, deep within you, will cause you to lose more sales than almost anything will.

First, that need, the desperation will be evident to your prospective customers before you get to the point to ask for the sale. Prospects will notice your intensity and nervousness when you attempt to set an appointment or conduct a sales presentation. Then, as you begin to ask for the order, that fear and anxiety will act like a warning beacon and customers will avoid you like the plague.

As this continues, the more it looks like the sale and the money is slipping away, the more desperate you become. The more desperate you become, the more the sale slips away and the more desperate you become. You must be able to put the sale and the commission in their proper perspective.

Please don't misunderstand; that desperation does not have to be in the form of a sad or frightened face. Actually, it usually comes with a great big smile. Here's an example:

"Have I Got A Deal For You!"

You are walking though the local mall, when you casually stroll into a clothing store. From the far side of the store, some 30 or 40 feet away, a sales person spots you as you come through the door.

He stops what he is doing and drops the things in his hands as his eyes light up as if he just saw a loved one come back from the dead.

He yells from across the store, **"Hey! How are you?! I'll be right there!"** He starts running towards you. Leaping over chairs, catapulting over tables and knocking down a few displays, he comes charging at you with a business card stuck to the front his forehead.

He catches you as you had begun backing up, grabs in a bear hug and proceeds to violently squeezes and shake your whole body as he insists, **"IT IS SOOOO GOOD TO MEET YOU...WHAT CAN I DO FOR YOU TODAY?!"**

How would you respond to that? If you are like most people, you would run out of that store or look for a mirror to see if the word "SUCKER" is spelled out on your forehead.

That example may be overdramatized a bit, but I think you know what I mean.

You would have to wonder why in the world is this total stranger so overjoyed to meet you, and the answer is obvious. You have to feel that the sales person's joy will somehow come at your expense. He wants your money. When you get desperate for the money, your mannerisms will change and people will notice.

When you become desperate for money, it does not always materialize as fear and nervousness; often it shows up as excessive kindness. You become overly, unnaturally nice and accommodating.

People are not stupid. They can tell when you are being nice and bending over backwards because you want their money. People can discern the person who will do anything to make a sale, and that person is dangerous.

So what do you do when your stress is real and you cannot hide it? You must be able to put the sale in its proper perspective. Here is how to do just that.

The Proper Perspective

Let us assume that you are in a difficult and stressful financial position. You have not closed a sale in weeks or months. To say that money is tight would be the understatement of the year.

Your spouse is getting anxious and beginning to hint that perhaps it's time you got a new job, a *real* job. Everything is going haywire, nothing is working right and the bills are piling up. You need funds and you need them now.

You have been working harder and harder, making more calls, trying to set more appointments. Now you have an appointment and the possible sale is a rather sizable one.

If you close this sale, your net commission will be nearly $1,500. You know that $1,500 will change your entire life at this moment. In your situation, that $1,500 is the equivalent of a million bucks.

If you close the sale, you will be able to pay the rent or mortgage, make the car payment, keep the electricity turned on and even have enough left over to get your daughter a birthday gift just in time.

You *need* this sale. You really need this sale. At a moment like this, it becomes impossible for you not to develop a tremendous amount of anxiety about this upcoming sales interaction. Let's face it; this is a very important sales call! This is a critical sales call.

Actually, *everything* relies on how well you do on this presentation. This one, single sale is the most important thing in the world right now. If you are successful and you close the sale, then life goes on. Whew!

However, if you do not close this sale, then who knows what could happen. You might be evicted. Maybe you and your family will be homeless.

Perhaps the state may take custody of your children. My goodness, if you don't close this sale, life as you know it is over!

What I want you to note here is that when the need for money is critical (and let's face it, sometimes it is), you will put all of the weight on the outcome of the sale.

Simply put, the sale is worth $1,500 and $1,500 will save your life. You will either gain or lose $1,500 on this sales call. That $1,500 is everything.

When you feel like this, it is impossible for the pressure not to radiate from you, and all of the psychology in the world will not change that. It is an enormous amount of pressure. So how in the world do you not feel this pressure or let it show?

Please prepare to take some notes or put the highlighter to work here. I am going to explain exactly what you need to do to get your mind off the money when you are in a selling situation. I can tell you that it does not have anything to do with some psychological mind games or hyping yourself up.

I know you have heard people say or have had your sales management tell you things like:

"Don't worry about it...every NO gets you closer to a YES!" "Just put it out of your mind...think positive!"

I also would imagine that every time you hear things like that when you are in hot water, you think, "Hogwash!" or much worse. No. What follows has nothing to do with positive thinking; it is about reality.

What is the Sale Worth?

To get your mind right and to get your emotions in check, you have to first understand exactly what the sale, that big sale and the commission, is really worth. You have to figure out the actual, true amount that the sale will give you.

What you must come to understand is that the sale, in our example, is not worth $1,500. Your commission is not $1,500. You will not be paid $1,500 if you close the sale. You will not lose $1,500 if you do not close the sale.

You may be thinking that is not true; your commission is indeed $1,500 and that is how much is at stake. No.

This sale, and every sale, is only worth the incremental value of a *single sales call*. That's all. The sale is only worth to you the incremental value of a single sales call. So, what is a single sales call worth?

Consider this; you will make $1,500 when you close the sale. Okay. However, do you close every sales call you attempt? Do you sell every prospect you try to close?

The sale is only worth the incremental value of a single sales call.

Of course, you do not. You do not close every sales call you make. So, what do you make when you do a sales presentation and you do not close the sale?

The general thought is that you do not make anything. However, this is not true.

Let us look at your numbers, your actual performance statistics over a period of time. Let us look at your sales metrics, the science of your selling.

As we do that, let us assume we see that your closing average is 20%. That is, that over time, we can see that you have historically closed at a pace of 20%.

You sell or close 1 out of every 5 closing attempts. You close 1 out of every 5 presentations, so you have a closing percentage of 20% (1 divided by 5 = .20).

With that, there have been times when you have closed 3, 4 or 5 sales in a row. You have even closed multiple sales in 1 day before. However, you have also had times when you went for a few weeks and did not close anything. When you average it all out, you have closed 20% of those that you have attempted to close.

From your records, from your actual performance data, we also see that when you close or make a sale, your average commission has been $1,000. On an average, you have made $1,000 when you close a sale.

With that, you have had some big sales where you made $1,500 or $2,000 and you have even closed a sale for $3,200 commission once.

However, you have also had many sales where you made less than $500. When you average it all out, on average you earn $1,000 commission on every sale you make. Does that make sense?

Now let's put these two facts together.

We know that you make $1,000 on the average when you close 1 sale, and that it takes you 5 presentations to close that 1 sale. Therefore, since it takes you 5 presentations, 5 people to try to close, in order to close 1, then in actuality, you EARN one fifth (1/5th, 20%) of the whole every time you attempt to close. Does that make sense?

Every time you conduct a complete presentation and ask for the order, you earn one fifth of the pay off, regardless of if you are paid at that moment or not.

When you ask for the order, you earn the incremental portion of the whole payoff in accordance with your closing average.

If you are paid $1,000 when you sell, and it takes you 5 presentations to sell, then you earn $200 each time you do a presentation.

It is imperative that you understand this, and we will get deeper into it in the next chapter.

In this example, you will make $200 every time that you do a presentation and ask for the order, regardless if that particular prospect buys or not.

Every prospect does not buy, only 1 out of 5 prospects buy. So, with those who do not buy, you still earn 1/5 of the sale.

One of the five will buy and you will get the full pay-off of the $1,000 in a lump sum. However, you *earn* 1/5 with every presentation.

It does not matter which prospect buys and which does not. Every complete sales presentation that you do earns you $200, period. Although you are paid in one large chunk for all 5 presentations, **this is still how you actually EARN the money.**

Further, you still only earn $200 per closing attempt, even though the sale that you are working on at the time is worth $1,500. Remember, your average sales commission is $1,000 and that takes into account those sales that earn you much more and much less. Either way, you average $1,000 per sale, and therefore you average $200 per closing attempt.

The bottom line is that this huge sale, this life-saving close is not worth $1,500. It is only worth $200. Period. Please understand that this is not a mind game; it is the truth.

When you understand this, then you can relax. This next sales call is not worth $1,500. The most it is worth is $200. Not only that, but

You are going to earn $200 from this presentation regardless if the prospect's buys or not!

So you have no need to feel any pressure whatsoever. Not only does this one single sales call not cause you to risk everything, you actually risk nothing. You can relax because that one sales call, that little $200 is not going to solve all of your problems. However, you had better hurry up and get going to another sales presentation so that you can earn another $200!

If you had this mindset the entire time, you would have been calm the entire time. You would have been confident the entire time. You would know that it does not matter if this prospect buys or not, you still make $200 regardless.

Keep in mind, however, that these numbers, these averages, only work when you put forth your best effort on each sales presentation.

So you cannot think that you can give a half-hearted effort on some, because others will buy. Each has to be your best effort or you mess up the averages.

Our example used $1,000 average sales commission and a 20% closing average. But what are *your* numbers?

How much do you actually make for every closing attempt you make? Figure out your numbers and put the sale in its proper perspective.

Think about this: Imagine that I were to go with you on your sales calls or sat by your side as you hammered the telephone. As I shadowed you, I had a huge wheelbarrow full to the brim of crisp $50 bills with me.

Every time that you completed a sales presentation and asked for the order, I gave you one crisp $50 bill. I am going to give that money to you regardless of if the prospect says yes or no.

I am going to pay you $50, or $100, or $425, whatever is the amount of your personal average, right on the spot every time you simply *attempt* to close a sale. Every time you just ask for the order, regardless of if the prospect buys or not.

If that were the case, how many closing attempts would you make every day? How many would you do in a week? I would image that the figure is a lot more than you do right now.

Also, if I were to pay you a few hundred dollars, or even $50 or $20 every time you did a sales presentation, if you had a presentation that ended badly, where the prospect hung up the telephone or threw you out the door, what would you do?

Would you sit there, sulking that you lost a big sale? Would you go crazy over not being able to overcome the objections? Would you analyze the situation for weeks? Or would you simply run out as quickly as possible and do another sales presentation, knowing that you get paid either way?

It is imperative that you get this and ingrain this understanding deep down in your mind and in your heart. It is the truth.

In addition, once you get this understanding deep in your head, something magical happens. Once you truly understand that the sale at hand means pretty much nothing, then all of the pressure leaves you and therefore leaves the prospect. The prospect can tell that you are not desperate for the sale.

The magic that happens then is that when you begin to push, when you start to persist, the prospect can feel that your persistence is not because you need the money. Your persistence is not self-centered.

Now add your true belief in the product or service that you are selling, and the customer can feel that you are pushing because you believe in your heart that it is best for them. The buyer can feel that you are pushing because you care about them and have their best interest at heart.

That is the moment when you become more than *just* a sales person to the prospect. That is when you become a partner, a professional consultant and trusted advisor.

Get your mind off the money and the
money off your mind.

Semester Review
CHAPTER 4
A = Ask

1. Unbelief in what you sell and the purpose of what you do will prevent you from being able to ask for the order with strength and conviction.

2. Your need for the money will come through as you ask for the order, forcing the prospect to distrust you.

3. Your lack of superior knowledge of what you sell and of your industry will prevent you from asking for the order with strength and conviction.

4. To maintain your focus and to get the money off your mind, you must put the sale in its proper perspective.

5. The sale is only worth the incremental value of a single sales call.

6. You earn that incremental value on every closing attempt, regardless of the outcome of the sale.

Semester Assignments

1. You must figure out what you earn on your *average* sale. How much commission do you earn on average? If you do not have accurate data to do this, then ask your sales management for the average sales commission for most sales people with the firm.

2. You must then take that to the next level and figure out exactly how much you earn on every sales call, presentation, demonstration or any time when you ask for the order. You have to calculate much you earn when you attempt to close, even when the prospect says, "No."

CHAPTER 5

S = S.O.S: The Science of Selling

Contrary to popular belief, selling is not an art. Selling is also not a practice. Selling is first and foremost a science. Selling is a science that is often practiced. Selling is a science that is only rarely practiced by a sales artist.

Selling is a science and once you understand the nature of the science you can literally guarantee your success. The Science of Selling (S.O.S.) is the understanding of the mathematical logic and reasoning of your profession. It is the numbers; the equations, the math that supports the foundation of what you do. It is using your sales metrics like tools and as the building blocks to success.

SOS is the meat, the core of everything that you do. If you are to be truly exceptional in the world of selling, then you must develop a deep, an intimate understanding of SOS.

A PhD in sales demands a thorough understanding of the Science Of Selling. With that, the first step in understanding SOS is to understand exactly how you are paid.

How You Are Paid

You need to understand exactly *how* you are paid. By that, I do not mean how you receive your pay or what your commission structure is. I am referring to how you EARN your money and what your time is worth.

You got an introduction to this concept and understanding in the last chapter, but now it's time to break this open and get down to the core.

There are certain numbers, figures and facts that you must understand and keep track of. You must understand these sales metrics:

1. Your closing average
2. The amount of your average sale
3. Your average commission or compensation per sale
4. Your appointment setting average (if applicable)
5. Your contact rate (if applicable)

6. Exactly how many telephone calls you make every day or week

7. Exactly who many people you talk to every day or week

8. Exactly how many emails you send out, how many doors you knock on, how many calls you answer, etc., etc.

You must have detailed information, metrics as to every sales related activity that is applicable to your business.

You then need to be able to attach an exact dollar figure, not only to every sale, but to every sales call and every metric. You need to figure out not only how much you earn on an average sale, but what you earn when you DO NOT sell.

For instance, after some research, you find that you have a closing average of 20% or 1 out of 5. You also know that you earn on average $400 commission per sale. Keep in mind that these figures are averages compiled over a length of time. There are times when you may make three or four sales in a row, or close a sale for $1,000 or more in commission. However, over time, it averages out to 1 sale for every 5 closing attempts and $400 in commission.

Now consider this; if you make $400 for every 5 sales presentations or closing attempts, then you effectively EARN one fifth or $80 for each attempt. Remember how important this is.

You have to understand that when you <u>do not make the sale</u>, you still earn $80.

When you do not close the sale,
you still earn an incremental
amount of your average commission.

Now you can relax and go to work without worrying about closing each and every sale. Just complete your number of sales presentations (of course giving each your best effort) and do not worry about who buys and who does not.

This is also how you set goals and how you write your own paycheck. If you been in the world of selling for any length of time, you have no doubt heard phrases like,

✓ "In sales you can write you own paycheck…"
✓ "In sales you can make as much money as you want."
✓ "In sales you are only limited to how hard you work."
✓ "You can be your own boss…"

You have heard these sentiments or perhaps it was those very ideas that pushed to into a sales career in the first place.

However, after you have been around for a while, I will bet that you found it hard to find anyone who could actually show you exactly how to write your own paycheck. You have not had one sales manager or so-called sales guru who could sit down and describe precisely how you write your own paycheck, short of telling you just to work harder.

Well, not only am I going to describe to you in detail exactly how to write your own paycheck, but I am going to give you a mathematical formula to do so. Are you ready?

Understanding How to Write Your Own Paycheck

First, you have to know those numbers that I mentioned earlier. You have to know them and understand all of your metrics for a fact. These cannot be numbers based on guesswork or your feelings. You must have actual empirical data of past performance.

You may be thinking that it seems almost impossible to keep track of every single activity over a long period of time. How in the world can you track every single phone call, every contact and everything else? It would be impossible keep accurate records of your performance.

That is almost correct. Keeping such data is impossible to do without specialized software that you must have. Yes, if you are going to be a professional, if you are going to earn a PhD in sales, then you must learn to use certain industry specific computer applications.

You will learn what Customer Relationships Management is all about and become an expert CRM user. We will get into that in the next chapter.

You have to have real data and not numbers that you or anyone else made up. Now, if you are new to the world of selling or if you are new to the company that you are now working with, then seek out your sales management.

You need to go and ask your sales manager or supervisor to supply you with real performance data for sales people who are new to the company.

What is the closing average for a new sales person with this company? What is the appointment setting average? What are the average sale and the average commission?

****************IMPORTANT NOTE*****************

If for whatever reason, your management team cannot supply you with such detailed, proven, written and recorded data; then you should take that as a very serious cause for concern.

If your management makes guesses at this information or gives you wide ranging figures, I would be a little leery of this company.

If they do not know these numbers, then how did they come up with a commission structure and or a salary base to pay you? If your management team does not have actual performance data, then where did they get the things that they told you that you could do with the firm?

If management does not know these figures, then how do they know that you or anyone else can be successful with the firm?

They told you that you could make all this money and win prizes and all sorts of great things, right. Okay. Then where are they getting those figures?

They are guessing. They are guessing and they want you to risk your mortgage to see if you can prove them right.

Unfortunately, this type of management is far too commonplace in our industry. A company gets a product or service, hires a bunch of unsuspecting, bushy-tailed and starry-eyed sales people, and throws them out in the street with the hopes that they can make a living. If they do, that's great. If not, oh well.

Get with a company that knows what they are doing. You do not want to work with a firm that specializes in data that is purely PFA (Plucked From Air). Anyway, let's get back to it.

**********END NOTE**********

Get the statistical data from your sales management and then keep track of your own performance metrics as you go. Once you have the data, then you can write your own paycheck and that means to decide what you want to be paid and go and get it.

In explaining how to write your own paycheck, it is best that I illustrate the point to make it clearer. So, let's take a hypothetical sales person I'll call Johnny Gogetter. Now, Johnny has performance data that shows that he has a closing average of 20% and that he makes $200 per sale, on the average.

Johnny decided that he wants to earn $1,000 in commissions next week. That is, he wants to make $1,000 in addition to the $250 per week he gets in base salary. So, Johnny sets a goal to make $1,000.

His plan is simple; to make the $1,000 he needs to close 5 sales. He sets his goal to make 5 sales. That makes sense, right? He makes $200 per sale, close 5 sales = $1,000. That's it. That is his goal. Let's take a look and follow Johnny for that week.

Monday

On Monday, Johnny gets in the office bright and early as he is excited and can't wait to get started on his great week. He is full of optimism and expectation. He gets out to his first already scheduled appointment and closes it. The sale will net him $250. He gets to his second pre-set appointment, and low and behold, he closes it too; another nice one, $300. He has a third appointment, that he doesn't sell, but no problem.

Tuesday

Johnny gets in a little later and spends sometime at the water cooler telling everyone about the terrific day he had Monday. But he eventually gets out and makes a presentation and closes it, for another $150. He then has a referral from one of the sales on Monday, and closes it and it's a big-un, $400! He gets back to the office, and acts as if he is making cold calls, but doesn't actually get much done.

Wednesday

Johnny is on fire. He's already surpassed his goal of $1,000 and he is sure he will break the office record this week. However, he does linger around the office and deals with paper more than people. But hey, he has to take care of the paperwork for all those sales. He does manage to get out and get in one presentation, with no sale but that's no problem. He then catches up with his friends at the local pub for a mid-week Happy Hour brew-break.

Thursday

Thursday, Johnny gets his head back on straight, as he wants to finish the week with a bang. He hits the phones hard and sets 3 strong appointments from his list of referrals.

He gets out there and the first one goes flawlessly. He closes the sale for $200 commission. He does another referral, with no sale.

Friday

Johnny has that last referral set for first thing in the morning and he nails it, $250. He has one appointment he made from a cold call, but he thought it was weak. He gave it a half-hearted attempt and no sale. Johnny calls it a day, even though it's only 1:30 in the afternoon, and takes a well-deserved early weekend.

Wow. So what do you think about Johnny's week? Do you feel that he had a good week? Johnny is sure ecstatic.

Johnny greatly exceed his goal of earning $1,000 in commissions. He made a whopping $1,550 that week. He closed 7 sales instead of 5.

Question:

What do you think? Was that a good week?

Answer:

It may shock you to know that actually, our hero Johnny Gogetter had the worst week he could have had. It was so bad that it may end his relationship with that company and possibly end his sales career.

Say whaaaaaat?!! Let me explain why Johnny had such a horrible week.

First, Johnny closed 7 sales out of only 9 presentations. Okay, so what in the world is wrong with that? He was on a hot streak that week. What's wrong with that?

What's wrong with that is that 7 out of 9 is just about an 80% closing average. Johnny's closing average cannot support that. Johnny's closing average is 20%. His average is only 20% and he closed at an 80% pace.

What is wrong with that is that Johnny's real closing average will eventually come true! It has to. It is the law. Now what do you think has to happen for his closing average of 20% to come true?

A Flip of the Coin

Look at it this way. A regular two-sided coin, when flipped, will average landing on heads 50% of the time and tails 50% of the time. That is the averages. That is the law of averages.

The law of averages is like any other law…it will come true. Flipping a coin will eventually end up at a 50-50 split as to its landing on heads or tails. If you flip the coin 10 times and it lands on heads 8 out of that 10 times, what do you think is going to happen over the next 10 flips?

Of course, it is going to land on tails a disproportionate number of times to balance out the law of averages.

Johnny closed 8 out of 10 sales. What do you think is going to happen over the next couple of weeks? His averages are going to catch up with him and he is going to go into the tank.

This example is exactly what happens to average, undertrained sales person all over the world. This is why you see sales people with incomes that fluctuate wildly between feast and famine.

This is why you hear people say things like,

- ✓ "Don't get into sales; it's a crap-shoot."
- ✓ "Commissioned sales is a gamble every week..."
- ✓ "One week you got it, and one week you don't."

No, no, no. All of that talk is from those who think they are professionals, but are not.

Okay, then what could Johnny have done? After all, he did have a slew of hot referral leads, and they were buying. What was he supposed to do?

What Johnny was supposed to do is the same thing you and any other professional needs to do. You need to concentrate on the sales activities, on the metrics and not on the sales.

Johnny looked at his metrics and found that he made an average of $200 per sale and therefore he set out to make 5 sales.

However, what is far more important than the amount of the average sale, is his closing average. Johnny closes at 20%. Therefore, for him to close 5 sales, he should have completed 25 closing attempts.

While Johnny's goal was to make 5 sales, his goal should have been to make 25 attempts to close, or 25 sales presentations. His goal should have been to do 25 presentations and he should have set out to do those 25 presentations regardless of what happened on each. He should have *concentrated on the 25 sales interactions and nothing else.*

Should Johnny have set out to do 25 closing attempts, he would have sold the same 7 that he sold, and probably more; however, he would have kept the coin flipping! He would have kept working; he would have kept his averages in line with reality.

What you have to do is look at your closing average and set goals based upon reality. Set goals that are about selling activities; that are about performing a set number of presentations or closing attempts, or telephone calls or emails or whatever it may be. You cannot base goals on sales.

The sale is the result of a process. Therefore, you must set goals based on the integral steps in the process.

Let's take a peek back in on Johnny Gogetter and see what happens the following week.

Monday

Johnny is so sure of himself now that he has guaranteed his wife that he will be sales person of the year. He set a goal to make $1,500 in commissions again this week. He hits the streets full of expectancy and runs 2 more of those great referral appointments, but sells none. He manages to get in one more presentation and sells it, $150.

Tuesday

Johnny gets in real early as he is not playing now. He hits the phone hard and gets out in the afternoon and gets in 3 presentations! All 3 are no sale. He manages to get in a quick cold call and does a great presentation, but no sale. But, hey, it's only Tuesday.

Wednesday

Johnny gets out and puts in one of the hardest working days ever. He does 5 presentations and closes 1 for $200. Now Johnny is beginning to wonder what is going on. He is trying to figure out what is wrong. What is he doing differently this week from last week? It must be the presentation, he thinks. So he makes a few adjustments to his sales presentation.

Thursday

Nervousness and frustration begins to set in as Johnny fails to close on another 2 attempts. Then it hits him. He knows what is wrong. He realizes that last week he wore his other shoes.

He wore those other shoes all last week and most of the time he wore that tie his daughter gave him for Christmas. That's it! He needs to put back on those other shoes and wear that tie. That will get him out of this horrible slump.

Friday

Johnny pumps himself up. He is ready to *positively think* his way through the slump, plus he is wearing the right shoes and the right necktie…

As you can guess, this continues as Johnny spirals out of control and down the drain. For most people, that example should sound eerily familiar. It is exactly what happens.

Johnny is not in a slump. In fact, there is no such thing as a slump. It is simply Johnny's closing average catching up with him. Johnny is on the path the he set up for himself.

There is no such thing as a sales slump. Think about that coin again. You flip the coin 10 times and it lands on heads 8 out of the 10 times. You keep flipping and the next 10 times it lands on tails 8 out of 10 times.

> There is no such thing as a "sales slump." An unusually long drought in sales is always due to an inconsistent work ethic.

Do you think that something is wrong with the coin during the times it is landing on tails repeatedly? Do you think, "Oh, this coin is in a slump, something is wrong." Do you think that maybe your flipping technique has changed?

No. You realize that it is only natural for it to land on tails more because it landed on heads more before. It's the law of averages.

However, instead of understanding this, Johnny, like so many millions of sales people; begins to change his presentation or some other staple of what was a very successful sales process.

Now, the averages are completely thrown out of whack because he is no longer doing the same presentation! Now the historical data, all of those numbers, all of his sales metrics, no longer make any sense.

Then fear sets in and he begins to get superstitious and starts wishful thinking. He thinks about his clothes and if having a big breakfast has something to do with when he sells or not.

Fear becomes more evident and he starts to get desperate. His wife is freaking out and he starts to feel the pressure to close a sale. Are they going to be able to make the car payment this month? Are they going to lose the house?

By the third week, that need for the sale is written all over his face. Prospective customers can sense his desperate motives and begin to not trust him, making it even harder to close a sale. The harder it is to close, the more desperate he becomes, and the more desperate he becomes, the harder it is to close.

I have seen this type of a great hot-streak, this kind of a *great week;* destroy the careers of far too many sales people, especially when it happens very early in the person's career.

The Formula for Writing Your Own Paycheck

For the formula to writing your own paycheck, you want to take all of the above and take it just one step further. Let's assume that some of your sales numbers are as follows:

Closing average:	20%
Average commission:	$250
Appointment setting average:	20%

Let's further assume that your goal is to earn $1,000 in commissions. Now you already know not to set a goal just to make 4 sales, right?

You know that in this case, you need to do 20 presentations or closing attempts. However, do not stop there. Take it one more step. You want to consider the *one sales metric that precedes your closing attempts.* Depending on what type of business you are in and your sales process, that activity will be different.

In this case, the activity that precedes the closing attempt or presentation is the telephone call that sets up the appointment.

In this case, we know that you need to complete 20 closing presentations; but how many telephone calls (the preceding sales metric) does it take you to set 1 closing presentation appointment?

Your appointment setting average on the telephone is 20% or again, 1 out of 5. Therefore, it takes you 5 calls to set 1 appointment. You need 20 appointments.

So you will need to make 100 telephone calls to set those 20 appointments. You can break those down and make 20 phone calls every day, calling in the morning and running appointments in the afternoon.

Or you can make all of your calls or Mondays or Tuesdays and run the appointments the rest of the week. Any way that you do it, you just need to make certain that you complete 100 phone calls per week.

You then set out to complete those 100 phone calls no matter what. Your goal is not to make $1,000. It is not to make 5 sales nor is it to complete 20 presentations. Your goal is to make 100 phone calls! Period.

It was still very early in my career, while I was with Kirby Vacuum Cleaners where my close friend, Wesley Bates and I eventually opened a Kirby office that I began to understand this science.

The way I out sold my peers was that while I did indeed work harder, that work had a definitive purpose. I concentrated on one thing and one thing only, and that was to shoot for 5 complete Kirby demonstrations every day, and to never go home, under no circumstances until I did at least 3.

If there was enough time in the day and I had the leads, I would get in 5 demonstrations (demos). However, under no circumstances did I allow myself to go home until I did at least 3 demos and asked someone to buy that Kirby at least 3 times. NO MATTER WHAT.

I have done Kirby demonstrations that began after midnight and as early as 5:00 in the morning to people such as to nurses and others who worked odd hours.

While my counterparts concentrated on closing sales and closing the big sale, I simply did whatever I had to do to get in 3 to 5 demos every single day, which eventually gave me an average of 4.5 demos a day.

Of course, most of my fellow sales reps would say that their plan was to do X amount of demos every day; which was in fact Kirby's plan for sales reps. However, if most of them sold two machines in one day, that was usually the end of that day. For some of them, if they sold one machine, they quit.

For me, it didn't matter if I sold my first two demos; as far as I was concerned, I did not do my job until I did at least 3 demos. If I sold the first 3 and had could get in one or 2 more, I did.

Little did I realize that during that time, my closing average shot up from the Kirby plan average of 25% - 30% to a whopping 75% to 80% and still, I made sure to get in at least 3 demos every day.

My time with Kirby Vacuum Cleaners was perhaps the most valuable learning time of my career and gave me a rock solid foundation in direct sales.

Kirby provided the perfect example of what it means to work hard and follow a proven plan and I believe, to this day, Kirby may still be one of the best launching pads for a direct sales career.

The numbers will work. I can guarantee you that if the numbers in the example above were your actual numbers, and you set out to make 100 phone calls every week, and did that, and paid no attention to anything else; you would make so close to $1,000 every week, week in and week out, that you would think it was a guaranteed salary.

When you work like this, you work like a professional. As a professional, I don't get up and go to work thinking, "Oh, I hope I make a sale today." Or, "Gee, I hope I can make enough money this month to pay the bills."

If you go to work wishin' and-a-hopin' and-a-prayin that you have a successful sales week or month, then you are missing the boat.

You cannot rely on a lucky roll of the proverbial dice. Selling has nothing to do with good fortune, luck or happenstance. Selling is not sorcery. Selling is science!

A professional sales person, even on a straight, direct commission, should earn a well above average income that does not fluctuate much.

You must operate with deliberate precision and intent.

Pop Quiz

Q. If the above numbers were your numbers and you set out to make 100 appointment-setting telephone calls, how much would you earn every time you make one phone call?

A. When you make 100 calls, you set 20 appointments and you close 4 sales that average $250 each earning you a total of $1,000. Therefore for every 100 calls you make, you earn $1,000. Therefore, for every single phone call you make, you earn 1/100 or $10. Does that make sense?

Q. If you wanted to earn exactly $1,110, how many calls should you make?

A. You make 111 phone calls and see if you don't make almost exactly $1,110.

Please understand that this is not some armchair-executive theory. I have personally done this and lived by the Science of Selling my entire career. In fact, early in my career, I used to use SOS to recruit sales people.

That is how I grew to become such a successful sales manager and built widely successful sales teams.

As a District and Regional Sales Manager, 90% of my sales people were *personally* recruited by me or other sales people in my organization.

One way I did that was to issue a direct challenge to sales people that I met who were comfortable with the little salary they received from their company and were afraid of a straight commissioned sales position.

I was a sales manager with Gulf Industries Corporation (now Signtronix, Inc.), which offered one of the greatest direct sales opportunities for commissioned sales people in the world, and still does today.

On a rainy day, I'd walk into a store in a mall or onto a car lot or some other situation where sales people often wait until people come to see *them*.

There, I would run smack into sales reps that tripped over each other trying to get to what appeared to be, one of the best "ups" of the day.

After the heartbreak of finding out that I was not a potential customer, I would explain the sales opportunity that I and Signtronix could offer and invited him or her to come and check out my team. I would usually get the standard fear of a straight commission reply, to which I offered a challenge.

This sales person and I would make a written prediction on how much money we would each earn over the next pay period. The sales rep would include his or her salary and add in expected commissions and bonuses for the upcoming week, for example. I, in turn, would write down how much I expected to make. We would reconvene at the conclusion of the pay period, producing our respective paychecks or other proof of our earnings.

The wager was that if I came closer to my prediction, working on a straight commission, than they did with a salary, then they would come and spend a day with me in the field.

To this very day, I have never lost that wager. Not only have I always came closer (often to the dollar) of my prediction, but the amount of my earnings were always 3, 4 or 5 times more than the salaried sales reps'.

That is how I built *The John Landrine Dream Machine* in Southern California, which became the top selling sales region for the company in the world.

Just try this yourself. The accuracy of how this works will astonish you.

Again, it has to be your best effort on every phone call and on every appointment. But if you are working from real numbers, from actual, factual performance data; then you can indeed write your own paycheck to the nickel!

Incidentally, remember my *Beat-the-Boss* contest, and the question was did anyone every beat me? There were only two of my sales people who ever did that.

One was Mark Warnake. Mark was an accountant who had no sales experience. As an accountant, he followed the training and the numbers; I mean he took the SOS to heart. Mark beat me once.

The other was guy named John Mauriello, who after two years of trying, eventually beat me, and then began to beat me consistently. Not only had John become an expert in SOS, but also he had earned a PhD!

More Science

There are hundreds of other very effective and profitable ways to use this data and to use your sales metrics. You need to have an effective and efficient way to compile and manage the data and be intentional in keeping it current. This will require that you gain a good understanding of customer relationships management (CRM) and become an expert in using a good CRM software system.

CRM is not software. CRM is a method of managing data; a process of managing and handling clients and prospective customers.

You first learn and design your CRM methodology or process, and then you use a CRM software system to help you manage your CRM process. Does that make sense?

If that is not quite clear, and I suspect for many sales people it is not, then guess what your next 50, 70 or 100 hours of prolonged study and specialized education needs to concentrate on?

Get books articles, audios, videos and whatever it takes, but put in the time, *real* time, and learn CRM. That does not mean do a cursory internet search and read a few headlines. Understanding CRM, depending on what you know already, should take you a minimum of at least 40 to 50 hours of real learning and study.

Look at understanding CRM as the equivalent of at least 1 full college class or 3 to 5 course credits toward your PhD. Yes, it is a lot of work.

In the next chapter on I.T., we will briefly touch on CRM software systems, but it is a mere fraction of what you need to know.

When you get this down and get to the point of truly utilizing CRM and your sales metrics, you will have at your fingertips all of the knowledge and tools to fix absolutely any problem in your entire sales process that you can ever possibly have.

Understand that when sales are slow, the answer is not always due to the lack of closing sales. When sales slow down or begin to lag, the instinctive response by most sales people and sales management is to look at sales closing rates.

It seems to make logical sense: when sales go down, it has to be because of not closing enough sales, right?

Wrong!

In fact, usually when sales are lacking, it is not due to not closing enough sales. However, the normal response is to increase closing activity, see more people, and work harder.

If that doesn't do it, the next step is to look at adopting better closing techniques. What are the main objections that are preventing sales people from closing sales? How can we better overcome those objections?

Yes, sometimes the answer to the problem is working harder or seeing more people, as we just saw with Johnny. His numbers were way behind. If he stayed on point and worked his tail off, getting back up to speed with his number of closing attempts, he would eventually get things back together.

However, working harder and adopting better closing techniques are only a small fraction of the solutions to slow sales. Most of the problems, most of the more harmful problems, are more detrimental to the sales process and are much more difficult to identify.

The very worst problems that sales people and organizations suffer from the most, do not even exist as far as their victims realize.

The worst, most devastating problems to sales success is neither a lack of hard work nor bad closing techniques. Often the culprit is deep in the numbers and it takes a sales scientist, one with a PhD, to figure it out.

Get your highlighter ready again as I give you a way to uncover and solve problems that are invisible to 95% of sales people and organizations in the world.

It all starts by understanding your sales process.

What is Your Sales Process?

A hypothetical company I'll call ABC Software Systems, is very good at maintaining sales metric data and insists that all sales people use their in-house CRM system and they have done so for many years.

Over the years, they have compiled the metrics of what it takes a sales person to be successful with the firm. If a sales person diligently keeps up with these underlying statistics, they are sure to have a fruitful, rewarding and very lucrative career. Those numbers look like this:

ABC Software's
Weekly Sales Success Plan

Cold/Warm Calls:	100
DMs (Decision Makers) Reached:	60
Appointments Set:	15
Appointments Ran:	12
Proposal Appointments Set:	10
Proposal Appointments Ran:	8
Proposal Closes Attempted:	6
Proposals/Sales Closed:	2

Let's take a look at this. ABC says that for the *optimum* selling scenario, the optimum sales process, the plan should go like this:

As a sales person, you should make 100 cold and/or warm calls to set appointments every week.

Their records then show that your contact rate should be 60% as you should reach 60 DMs.

Of the 60 DMs you reach, you should set 15 appointments, of which 3 cancel, reschedule or something, and you should end up actually running 12 of those appointments.

Of the 12 appointments ran, you should set an appointment to make a proposal with 10 of those prospects; however, you will get back in to present a proposal only 8 times.

Of those 8 proposals, you will get to the point to actually ask for the order 6 times, of which you will sell 2 of them.

Now, of course, you can do better than this plan. You can make more calls or close at a higher rate or set more appointments than the numbers listed. However, you need to perform at least to the level in the optimum plan to ensure success.

Your Optimum Selling Scenario

This is exactly what you need to do for yourself. You need to figure out exactly what your optimum selling situation looks like.

If everything went exactly according to plan, what would happen? What is your plan? What is your company's plan?

You want to figure out your optimum plan, of course, making sure it stays within the confines of reality.

If the average closing rate in the firm is 15% and the top sales people in the history of your company have had a closing average of about 22%; then please don't put down your optimum plan with a closing average of 50%.

Use real numbers. In fact, be a little conservative. Use numbers that you can bank on. Start with the number of sales.

In your company, how many sales should you make every week or month to make a good, well above average income? How many sales does the average, long-term sales person make at your firm? How many sales *should* you make?

Then, how many presentations will it take to close that number of sales? What is a realistic closing average? How many calls do you need to make or emails do you have to send out or doors do you need to knock on to get those appointments?

Keep going like this until you get an optimum sales process for what you sell.

If you sell a number of products or services and each has a slightly different optimum sales process, then you can either create an optimum process for each, or average them out to get one that can represent them all.

Perhaps your sales process is a one-call close. If so, don't think that there is not a process involved. You still have to knock on a certain amount of doors and talk to a certain amount of people.

Let's say that you sell signs or advertising services to small businesses and you go door-to-door looking for business owners. You then find the owner, do a sales presentation and ask for the order, all right there within the span of an hour. Or perhaps you sell cable and internet services door-to-door and your entire presentation is 10 to 15 minutes on the doorstep. Okay.

Answer these questions:

1. How many sales do you need (or want) to make every week, on the average?

2. How many times must you ask for the order to get that number of sales? What is your closing average?

3. How many presentations must you make in order to ask for the order that many times?

4. How many owners or DMs do you need to talk to in order to get that many presentations? Every owner you talk to doesn't grant you a presentation; what is your presentation average?

5. How many doors do you need to walk into to meet that many owners?

Perhaps you work in telephone sales and you feel that since you have a one-call close on the phone, you do not have a sales process.

You do still have a very detailed sales process and you need to break down that telephone call. Again, start with how many sales do you need to make?

Then, how many times do you need to ask for the order to make that number of sales?

How many telephone presentations do you have to make to get to the point to ask for the order enough times to close enough sales?

Continue like this all the way to figuring out exactly how many times you need to dial the telephone. You have a process.

Let's get back to ABC.

ABC Software also has an optimum timeline built into their plan.

ABC Software's
Weekly Sales Success Plan

Sales Metric	#	Time
Cold/Warm Calls:	100	21 days
DMs (Decision Makers) Reached:	60	1 day
Appointments Set:	15	10 days
Appointments Ran:	12	1 day
Proposal Appointments Set:	10	5 days
Proposal Appointments Ran:	8	1 day
Proposal Closes Attempted:	6	1 day
Proposals/Sales Closed:	2	1 day

Let's look at this.

Cold/Warm Calls: 100   21 days

What ABC is saying is that when you have a lead; a referral, a cold call lead, a name in the database or whatever, that it should take you no more than 21 days to get to it and do something. You have to have gotten on the telephone and tried to make contact with the DM. A lead of any kind should not be sitting in your possession for a month without you doing *something*. Now, of course you do not make contact will all of the leads.

We know that you will only actually reach 6 out of 10 (60%), but on average, you should have made contact with that 60% within 21 days.

DMs (Decision Makers) Reached: 60   1 day

Then once you reach the DM, you should set an appointment in one day. You should set an appointment with the DM on that one call, right there on the spot when you have him or her on the telephone. Again, no one expects you to set an appointment with everyone you reach, but you should set one with 25% of them.

Appointments Set: 15   10 days

Once you have set the appointment, you should get in front of the prospect and consummate that appointment within 10 days. So, you should not be setting appointments 3 or 4 weeks out.

They should be set close, 10 days out max. You may only set appointments with 15 of the 60 DMs or 25%, but those appointments should be set within 10 days.

Appointments Ran: 12   1 day

Once on the appointment, you should set an appointment to present the proposal on the spot: 1 day. Of the 15 appointments you run, only 12 of them will get far enough along for you to set up a proposal, second or closing appointment and you should do that on the spot.

Proposal Appointments Set: 10   5 days

Now, with those 12 appointments you set up to present a proposal, 10 of them will agree to let you back in to present that proposal within 5 days of the last appointment.

Proposal Appointments Ran: 8   1 day

Of those 10 proposal appointments you set, on average only 8 of them held up for a proposal meeting.

Proposal Closes Attempted: 6   1 day

Of that 8, only 6 of them get to the point where you actually ask for the order. Of course, you do so there on the spot, but with 2 of those prospects you probably will not get to the point to ask for the order.

Proposals/Sales Closed: 2   1 day

Finally, of those 6 times you ask for the order, you close 2 sales, giving you about a 33% closing average or 1 out of 3.

Please remember, that this is an example only. Your process and your numbers will be very different. However, you need out figure out *your* numbers, figure out what is your planned optimum sales process including time frames.

Also take into consideration cancelations and no-shows. While we always try to minimize these numbers as much as possible, they are a fact of doing business.

Once you have these numbers in place, numbers mind you, that you have based on facts not fiction; then you will have control of your destiny.

Learn to Work Smarter Not Always Harder

Now that you have a solid sales process, let's look at one way you can use it to increase sales and solve problems.

Using our hypothetical company and sales process again, let's assume that these are the numbers:

ABC Software's
Weekly Sales Success Plan

Sales Metrics	#	Time
Cold/Warm Calls:	100	21 days
DMs (Decision Makers) Reached:	60	1 day
Appointments Set:	15	10 days
Appointments Ran:	12	1 day
Proposal Appointments Set:	10	5 days
Proposal Appointments Ran:	8	1 day
Proposal Closes Attempted:	6	1 day
Proposals/Sales Closed:	2	1 day

You then go to work and keep accurate records of your sales activity in the company's CRM. After a few months, we see that your sales are way behind.

Instead of closing the 2 sales a week or 8 per month that the plan says you could and should close, you are only selling about half of that, and sometimes even less.

Once again, the standard response to this is to work harder, see more people, and make more calls. However, we look and we see that you have been making as many, if not more than the prescribed 100 cold or warm calls every week.

Then it must be that you need to learn better closing techniques and how to overcome more objections. However, when we look there, we see that your closing average is also on par with the plan. You close about 33%. So what is the problem? You are making enough calls, you are apparently working hard enough and your closing average is on target too. What is wrong? What do you do?

Keep in mind, most sales people do not even have enough basic facts to know exactly how many calls they've made or what their true closing average is in the first place, and therefore they are completely blind to any of this. But let us fill in the rest of your numbers and take a look at this as *professionals* and see if we can figure out how to help this sales person. When we look at your numbers…

Your Personal Sales Metrics

Sales Metrics	#	Time
Cold/Warm Calls:	100	21 days
DMs (Decision Makers) Reached:	35	1 day
Appointments Set:	8	10 days
Appointments Ran:	6.4	1 day
Proposal Appointments Set:	5	5 days
Proposal Appointments Ran:	4	1 day
Proposal Closes Attempted:	3	1 day
Proposals/Sales Closed:	1	1 day

Let's put your numbers side by side with the plan.

	You	Plan
Cold/Warm Calls:	100	100
DMs (Decision Makers) Reached:	35	60
Appointments Set:	8	15
Appointments Ran:	6.4	12
Proposal Appointments Set:	5	10
Proposal Appointments Ran:	4	8
Proposal Closes Attempted:	3	6
Proposals/Sales Closed:	1	2

Can you spot the problem here? Actually, your numbers are exactly on target in every area except one. Let's add the actual percentages to the picture as that might make it a little clearer.

	You	%	Plan	%
Cold/Warm Calls:	100	100	100	100
DMs:	35	35%	60	60%
Appointments Set:	8	23%	15	25%
Appointments Ran:	6.4	80%	12	80%
Proposal App. Set:	5	80%	10	83%
Proposal App. Ran:	4	80%	8	80%
Proposal Closes:	3	75%	6	75%
Proposals/Sales:	1	33%	2	33%

As you can clearly see, the only area you are having problems is with the number of DMs reached. The plan says you should reach around 60% on the average. You only manage to reach about 35%. That is where the problem lies. In every other area, you are performing right on track. However, because you are off track in that one area, the result is that you close half of the sales and make half of the money. You are only closing half as many sales, even though your closing average is the same as the plan.

The problem is not closing. In this case, the problem is that when you get on the telephone to set appointments, you are not reaching enough DMs. The plan calls for you to reach 60%, but you are reaching only 35% of DMs.

Now think; why might that be? What could be causing this problem? What could make you have such a low appointment setting or contact rate?

The problem can very well be that you are not very good at getting past secretarial screens on the telephone. Does that make sense?

There could be other factors that can contribute to your low *call-to-contact* percentage. Perhaps your calling times are not best for your prospect demographic. As an example, maybe you call early mornings and you are calling attorneys, most of which are in court during that time of the day.

The point is your problem has nothing to do with what you and sales management thought.

How in the world is working harder and making more calls going to fix this? In fact, working harder and making more calls could actually make the problem worse!

How in the world is learning how to overcome more objections going to fix this?

Can you see what happens here? This is what most sales people and organizations do, and as the sales person works harder and longer and studies more and still does not see things get any better.

They then turn to superstitions, and a-hopin' and a-wishin' and before you know it...it's over. Our sales pro is now a cashier at the local convenience store.

Let's look at another example.

Here are the plan numbers side-by-side with your numbers.

Your Time   Plan Time

		Your Time	Plan Time
Cold/Warm Calls:	100	21 days	21 days
DMs	60	1 day	1 day
Appointments Set:	15	23 days	10 days
Appointments Ran:	6	1 day	1 day
Proposal Appt. Set:	3	5 days	5 days
Proposal Appt. Ran:	2	1 day	1 day
Proposal Closes:	1	1 day	1 day
Proposals/Sales:	0.5	1 day	1 day

At first glance, it seems you are doing everything right, but the result is only 2 sales a month instead of 8. Once again, there is only one area where you are failing, and that is with the time it takes you to get in the door when you set an appointment.

You reach the right amount of DMs, but you set up appointments too far away. Because of that, most of them never come through and you wind up actually only getting in front of 40% of the prospects (6) instead of 80% (12).

Again, how in the world is working harder going to solve this problem?

Can you see how and why most sales people and sales organizations have absolutely no clue as to what their problems are or how to solve them?

Having no idea as to what is actually happening they begin throwing mud up against the proverbial wall:

Let's try this…okay, that didn't work.

Let's try that…okay that didn't work.

All the while, the sales person is losing his or her shirt.

These were but a couple of generic examples of how to use your sales metrics and how to understand the metrics of your business.

***************IMPORTANT NOTE***************

Also note that if you are just starting out in keeping track of your numbers and figuring out your daily metrics, as you begin to set up your goals, do not look to try and catch up with the past.

If you look and notice that your goal should have been to do 10 demos every week, but you can see that over the last few months you only averaged 8, do not try to make up the demos that you have missed.

Start fresh right now. Start over again today. Also, if you, for whatever reason, end up falling too far behind, do the same thing; start fresh.

As you may have already guessed, when you do that, it will probably take you some time before your numbers begin to fall back in line.

True. However, just keep that in mind and start the coin flipping over from the beginning.

**********END NOTE**********

At any rate, if you want to be a true professional, if you ever want to operate at the top level in the industry, if you want to earn a PhD in sales, then you need to become an expert with these numbers. You have to become a scientist in the science of selling!

Become Street Wise

I'll conclude this semester with a concept that I believe will better help you keep this understanding close to your heart. If you can truly adapt the understanding of SOS and use it to write your own paycheck, it will revolutionize your career...almost instantly.

I shared this philosophy, this way of thinking, with all of my sales people and it became our own private language. The terms that we used on a daily basis, were known only to us, and they all had powerful and profound meanings.

The concept is that as you work, whether that be on the telephone, door-to-door, or making appointments and doing proposals, no matter what your working situation is, consider the field, your operational playing ground as *The Street*.

As you develop your own personal goals and daily tasks, you consider those as your job; they are the personal obligations that you must perform every day.

For example, let's say that you need to complete 5 presentations every day or 25 per week, that is your daily duty. That is what you have to do; it is the fee that you must pay the field. It is like a toll. It is what you have to pay The Street. Every day you must pay The Street.

Likewise, The Street must pay you. The Street owes you. The Street must reward you with 1 sale every day or 5 sales per week, but only when you have put in the required number of activities, the correct number of presentation/demonstrations.

If you do your job and complete 5 demos a day or 25 per week, then you do not owe The Street. You are even. Likewise, if The Street pays you 5 sales in return, it does not owe you and you are even.

However, if you fall behind on your numbers, if your numbers are in deficit, then you owe the Street. You never ever want to be in this position.

Consequently, if you have invested the correct activities and The Street did not pay you in the proper amount of sales and commissions; then The Street owes you, and that's okay, because it will always eventually catch up and pay you back.

This became a way of talking for the *Landrine Dream Machine*, as you would hear sales people talking and saying things like,

"So, how are you with The Street?"
"Oh, I'm good. Yes, I'm on time…"

"Well, I owe The Street 2, but I'm going to make those up today, so I'll be on track."

"The Street owes me big time! I'm waiting for a huge pay off!" With that, I will leave you this:

"If The Street owes you, you can celebrate.
The Street will always pay you back with huge bonuses.

However, if you owe The Street, be afraid.
The Street will collect with interest and penalties!"

Never owe The Street, my friend!

Semester Review
CHAPTER 5
S = S.O.S: The Science of Selling

---

1. Selling is science, not sorcery. Selling has nothing to do with luck. Selling is not primarily a practice or an art. Selling is first, and foremost a science. Selling is a Science that is sometimes practiced. Selling is a science that is rarely practiced by a sales artist.

2. A professional sales person, even on a straight, direct commission, should earn a well-above average income that does not fluctuate much.

3. You must learn your own personal S.O.S. The data and metrics have to be based on facts, not fiction. You cannot rely on numbers that are PFA (Plucked From Air)

4. You must develop an optimum sales process. Such a process must be exacting and based on actual performance data.

5. You must understand CRM. CRM is a process for managing prospects and customers. You must then

learn to use CRM software to manage your CRM process.

6. You have to begin to work smarter rather than just harder. You must *learn* how to work smarter as it is not something that comes natural. You have to understand how to fully use your numbers to uncover problems in your sales process and learn how to fix them.

Semester Assignments

1. Design your sales process. You need to break down your optimum sale into individual steps and include time frames if applicable.

2. Figure out your own personal numbers to write your own paycheck. Design a formula that is unique to you and your past sales performance data. Figure out exactly how many calls you need to make, how many doors you need to knock on, how many demonstrations you have to do and how many people you have to talk to every single day.

CHAPTER 6

I = I.T.: Information Technology

If you are going to be a professional today in almost any industry, you must become proficient with today's technology. In sales, it is imperative that you become an expert-level or at least an advanced-level user with certain technology. I'm sorry, but you simply cannot and will not become an expert, a true professional, or earn a PhD without it. Your first step in the area of technology has to be in CRM.

CRM Software

If you are still using Post-It Notes, paper, spreadsheets, a cell phone or PC calendar, 3" x 5" cards, or your magnificent memory to do business, you are a dinosaur living in the present awaiting extinction.

Customer Relationship Management (CRM) software is mission critical. You must first learn and understand exactly what is CRM and then learn how to use a sophisticated database management software system such as ACT!, SalesLogix, Goldmine or Salesforce.com or something. These programs are pre-designed and configured, relational database management systems.

I do not mean that you need simply to learn to use one of these programs. I mean you need to become an *expert*. Go to school, take classes online, do whatever you have to do to learn to maximize the power of a relational database management system.

All those numbers that we have been talking about are critical pieces of information that you have to keep track of and integrate with other data.

Do not try to do any of this in your head, please. I don't care how much of a genius you think you are, it is simply not possible.

Do not try to create some type of spreadsheet in Excel or an Access database either. It is not possible. Unless you are a program designer with advanced level skills and certifications in SQL DBA, SQL Server and database Access Application Development, then use a predesigned, sales-ready CRM database management program.

Understanding CRM and using a good system is about more than tracking leads and being able to remember appointments.

CRM will make you money. CRM will make you more money than any 1 or 100 sales can ever make you.

The only thing greater than the amount of money that good CRM will make you, is the amount of money you will *lose* by not using good CRM.

I know there are those who think that using CRM and putting so much information into the system is a waste of time. You may feel that the amount of time you would have to spend to put in your information and record your activities is too much and not worth it.

If you feel that way, first do not be ashamed, because you are not alone. This area is one where most sales people fail miserably. Consequently, this area is usually the *primary reason* why most sales people fail.

If you feel that daily data upkeep in a CRM is too much time or work or a waste of your time, it is because you do not yet understand the role and purpose of CRM.

For this, I fault management, as the average sales management team does not truly understand the use, purpose, or true value of CRM themselves, so they cannot and do not properly explain it to their sales teams correctly.

So allow me to set the record straight. Let me explain what the primary reason and purpose of CRM is. In doing so, let me first explain what the main purpose of your CRM is NOT.

The *primary* purpose for your CRM is NOT:

- ✓ To record your activities
- ✓ To keep track of appointments
- ✓ To keep track of birthdays and events
- ✓ To keep a record for the company to use when you leave
- ✓ For the company to keep track of your time
- ✓ For the company to keep track of your customers
- ✓ For your company to use against you when the need arises

Now with that said, I will admit that there are some organizations and management teams who have no clue as to the true meaning and value of CRM, and they often *do* use CRM for some of those short-sighted, outdated, ignorant reasons listed above.

However, the true purpose of CRM is to help you...

"Maximize productivity through proficient efficiency."

That is to maximize productivity through proficient efficiency.

In other words, CRM is to help you become more productive (your ability to produce large amounts of sales), by being proficient (become a skilled expert) at being efficient (achieving maximum productivity with the minimum expense, without wasting time or effort).

Put yet another way; the main purpose of your CRM is to help you make the most money with the least amount of effort.

If that doesn't interest you, then you are in the wrong business.

As a sales consultant and trainer, I used to acquire new sales company clients by telling the sales management team something like this:

"I will increase your sales by 50% to 100% literally overnight (within a week or so) without bringing in 1 new prospective customer and without increasing your sales averages or increasing your workload."

I have doubled a company's sales simply by exposing, and then plugging the holes in their prospecting process.

I hope that in the last chapter, I have already convinced you how bad you need good CRM, but just in case I have not, stay tuned.

You saw in the last chapter, S: SOS = Science Of Selling, the examples we used and how we applied the numbers to expose key problems and issues that, without good CRM, are impossible to detect, let alone fix.

Let me take you back to part of the chapter for a moment. Do you remember this?

		Your Time	Plan Time
Cold/Warm Calls:	100	21 days	21 days
DMs	60	1 day	1 day
Appointments Set:	15	23 days	10 days
Appointments Ran:	6	1 day	1 day
Proposal Appt. Set:	3	5 days	5 days
Proposal Appt. Ran:	2	1 day	1 day
Proposal Closes:	1	1 day	1 day
Proposals/Sales:	0.5	1 day	1 day

If you recall, in this situation, the sales person sets 15 appointments, but sets them so far into the future that many cancel or are lost. Of the 15 appointments, the rep actually only gets to complete 6 appointments, leaving 9 unaccounted for.

These are 9 prospective customers who were interested at least to the point of setting up an appointment. What happened to them?

What happens to yours? You may be thinking that you do not have any lost leads. However, how would you know? Let me ask you a couple of questions. Here is a quick quiz for you.

CRM Quiz

Please write your answer in the space below the questions. If the question does not apply to your selling situation, put N/A.

Q: When you set an appointment, do you have a fail-safe method or an *auto-alert* to make sure you call to confirm the appointment at the appropriate time? If so, what is it?

Q: How can you discern accounts/prospects/leads that have rescheduled an appointment more than once?

Q: How many account/prospect/lead classifications do you have? What are they? Are all of your leads classified simply as "leads?"

Q: How can you tell the difference between an account/prospect/lead that you did not get a chance actually to ask for the order, and one where you asked but did not sell?

Q: In the above question, is such a lead classified as a "No-Sale" or a "Dead" lead? Is it still classified as a lead at all?

Q: How many sales stages do you have in your sales process?

Q: What is the optimum time frame for your sales process from the time you get the lead to the time you receive money in your hand?

Q: How do you know if a sale, even though it closed, went beyond your plan time frame?

Q: If you find a sale that went longer or closed in a significantly shorter time than your plan, can you point to where and why it did so? If so, how?

Q: Do you have an automated, live task list manager? Does it prompt you and insist that you take care of important tasks?

Q: How do you know if you have missed an "Important" or "High Priority" call or task?

Q: If you miss or fail to complete a task that was scheduled on your task list as "Important," or "High Priority," what happens?

Q: Do you classify leads that are a no-sale into different categories according to the reason the prospect did not buy or according to the primary objection? If so, what are those categories?

If you answered "No," "I don't know," or if you stumbled in the least bit on just ONE of those questions, you are losing a ton of sales and a fortune in income.

Study, learn and understand CRM. Then get a good CRM system. **Bookmark this page.** When you begin to get into your CRM, come back and answer the above questions. You can also use the above questions as a guide to help you in choosing a CRM.

Choosing a CRM

There are hundreds of CRMs on the market today, and probably dozens that would fit your process. While I will not recommend one to you, I will give you some key things you may want to look for when choosing a CRM.

Incidentally, I began using database management systems well before they were even on the market. I created my own CRM database and used it for myself and for sales companies as a consultant back in the late 1980s and early 1990s.

Realizing how critically important it was to actively manage prospective accounts, I used an old program called Q & A which was a DOS-based, flat-file database by Symantec for the IBM PC.

I customized the program for sales people and at the time, what I provided for my clients may have been the precursor to modern day CRMs. I say that to say that I believe I can give you a good idea of what works and what does not.

First, remember that CRM is not software; it is the process that your software will manage. You must first have a sales process. Design that sales process like we did in the examples, or use your company's process and time frames. Once you have that, then you will look for a tool that will help you manage that process.

To find the most popular CRMs on the market, just get on any search engine and enter something like, "best CRM for sales people" or something to that affect, and start your research.

****************IMPORTANT NOTE***************

If you are not familiar with that last instruction, "get on any search engine..." or if you do not yet know how to do that, if you are computer illiterate, as they say; then I have some critical instructions for you.

First, close this book. Close this book immediately after finishing this note. Close the book and go and do whatever it is you have to do to learn computer basics. Go right now and do not come back to this book until you have done so.

You must learn the following basic computer skills:

1. Basic Windows
2. Basic word processing
3. Saving files
4. Basic email
5. Basic internet

Before you can even begin to think about the 5 Basic steps to a PhD, you need to learn the 5 basic steps to a PC. Otherwise, it is like trying to get a PhD before you enter elementary school. I am serous about this.

STOP READING RIGHT NOW.

You are fooling yourself to think that you will become a sales professional if you do not have basic computer skills. I'm sorry. When you have obtained these basic skills, come on back, and I'll be waiting.

Also, for those of you who are familiar with the basics, you know how to navigate Windows and get on the Internet, but you have never had professional training; I have a word for you too.

You may be thinking, "But I already know those things. I know Windows and the Internet and how to save a file…"

Please, please, please do not listen to yourself. Remember, at ExecuTrain Corporation, we were the largest technology training company in the world. Nearly every day we had to try to explain to a H.R. or I.T. director or other department head that most of the people in their department did not really know the programs that they were using and consequently were costing their company thousands or even millions of dollars.

The response was usually that they do not hear any complaints or anyone saying that they feel they need training. Of course not! Here is the problem...

If there is functionality or options that are available in the program that you are unaware of, then how can you possibly be aware that you are unaware of them?

You cannot possibly know that you do not know *what* you do not know.

Microsoft gave us some ammunition. Here are a couple of facts:

- ✓ The average desktop application user utilizes but 15% to 18% of the application's functionality.

✓ The average user in an office environment wastes approximately 3.5 hours a week in unproductive time fumbling around, trying to accomplish a task.

✓ Most desktop application users will increase their productivity from 30% to 50% from just one day of (beginning/introductory level) training.

Listen, I know you feel you are a MS Word or Excel expert. But I can also tell you that there is 75% of the program that you never even seen before. Please, take the time and go get professional training!

*********END NOTE**********

Company Provided CRM

First, your firm may have and use a custom or proprietary CRM, or an off-the-shelf one, or one that they recommend. Check out whatever they have first. If it is something that is built into your company's sales process and everyone else uses it, then it's a no-brainer; join your coworkers and do the same.

However, remember that often, management is unaware of the power and value of CRM, so they do not understand how to present the software or how to train people to use it.

Whatever training your company provides, go beyond that and seek out as much training on your company CRM as you can find. Become an expert-level user.

Industry-Specific CRM

You will find that most of the major CRM designers have custom versions of their CRM for specific industries. There are also CRMs designed exclusively for particular industries. You can find CRMs tailor-made for insurance sales people or real estate agents and brokers or for automobile sales professionals. If your firm does not provide or recommend a CRM, I strongly suggest that you pursue the option of selecting one customized for your industry.

Remember that you need to infuse your CRM with your personal sales process. You need to set up your database so that it reflects the particulars of how you sell. A CRM designed for your industry, already has taken these issues into account. They are already familiar with your sales process and how you work.

An industry-specific CRM will likely have built in provisions for the number of sales presentations you do, or if you make telephone calls to set up appointments, or if you have a financing step in your sales process, or the type of objections you receive and how your commission structure works.

If these types of things do not come already built into your CRM, then you need to customize what you have to make such options available. Can you do that?

Most people are not going to be capable of customizing or reprogramming an off-the-shelf CRM and therefore it is best to find something that closely aligns with your selling process.

A Few Things to look For When Choosing Your CRM

Here are just a few generic things you want to look for in choosing your CRM program.

1. **Live and Automated Task Management:** You want to make sure your system has a task manager, that is, a "To-Do List" that is automatically compiled every day and has built in alarms. As you work and enter sales data, the system should be able to separate all of your tasks. For example, if you set an appointment with ABC Company and you make a note to call to confirm the appointment

next week, the CRM should be able to add that task to your list and alert you when the time arrives to make that call. You should be able pull up a list of all of your tasks for the day, week, month, and longer with the click of a mouse. In addition, the CRM should record original calls and the results of that call being the appointment set.

2. **Detailed Contact Type:** Your system should be able to differentiate between the types of ways that you make contact with prospects and customers. Most will have at least 3 contact types:
    a. Telephone Call
    b. Meeting
    c. Email

However, you may need more than this. For instance, the CRM recorded that there was a telephone call at a certain date and time. However, did you call the prospect or did they call you? Depending on what you do, that could mean a world of difference to the account. It says Email. However, was it an incoming email or did you send one out? Also, you may need to include such methods of contact as texts, Facebook or other social media, Skype, etc.

3. **Sales Funnel Analysis:** You will need to be able to see how many prospects are at what point in your sales process at any given moment.

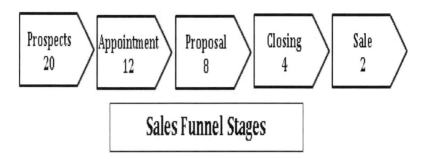

You want to know, for example, how many prospects or accounts are currently in the "proposal" stage and how many are in the "closing" stage.

Also, remember that *time line* or *time frame* we talked about? You need to know how long prospects have been at what stage. You need to know if you have prospects that get to a certain point in the process and then stagnate. How long did it take you to contact the client after you received the lead? How long did it take you to get back in front of the client to present the proposals after the discovery appointment? You need the ability to pull up reports that will allow you to see and analyze these metrics.

4. Sales Opportunity Probability Analysis: You also want a CRM that can provide you with accurate Probability Analysis. As you go along and create sales opportunities, you will note each potential sale as to what you believe the chances are that the sale will close. For instance, you may mark a strong referral lead with a 90% probability that you will make the sale. While a cold call lead, you may assign a 20% chance of closing.

Also, your probability scores should be tied to your plan statistics and performance metrics. When a prospect gets to the "Proposal" stage, for example, the system may assign an 80% probability of closing because data shows that you close 80% of the proposals you make. Your CRM should take all of this information as well as that from your sales funnel into consideration, and give you a prediction as to what you will close, when and for how much.

For instance, you may have 4 sales processes in the closing stage. One of the accounts has a near 100% probability of closing, one has an 80% chance and two are about 50%. Each of the possible sales average $1,000 in production.

Sales Funnel

Account 1:   100% = $1,000

Account 2:   80% = $1,000

Account 3:   50% = $1,000

Account 4:   50% = $1,000

You CRM will analyze this and tell you that you will close 70% or 2.8 sales and earn a total of $2,800.

Do not wrack your brain over this and as you can imagine, in real life the numbers will be exponentially more complex than this example. You will have accounts at varying stages in your sales process all with wide ranging probabilities of closing.

The point is that with a good sales process integrated with a sophisticated CRM, as a professional sales person, you know precisely, to the penny, what is happening in every moment of every given day.

As a professional, nothing should ever come as a total shock or surprise to you. You should never look up at the last minute and realize that your paycheck this week is going to be pennies. If you have a paycheck that is going to be short, you should have been able to see that coming weeks or even months ahead of time and been able to correct it.

5. Extensive Reporting Capabilities: Your system should be able to give you as many reports as you can literally imagine. There are basic reports that should be standard in every CRM. For instance, your CRM should have a *Dashboard or Quick View* or something that lets you see an overview of what is going on at a glance. Then, it should have basic reports such as Sales Forecasts, Pipeline Reports, Contact Reports, and Activity Reports.

However, you want access to more reports than you believe you will ever need, and some that you have never heard of nor understand as of yet, such as:

✓ Detailed sales process and call analytics
✓ KPI analytics
✓ Pipeline by stage
✓ Campaign revenue
✓ Sales by source
✓ And much more

If you have never used CRM and the one you are choosing has a bunch of reports that don't make any sense to you; that's a good thing.

Additional I.T. Tools You Need to Know and Use

In addition to becoming a CRM expert, there are several productivity and time management tools you need to know how to use. Here are but a few.

1. **Basic Windows:** Please, first learn the basics of Microsoft Windows. Like I said, I know that most people reading this are saying, "I already know how to use Windows!" And once again, I say perhaps you do not. It's a shame how many people do not understand actions and concepts such as saving and managing files, cut and paste, opening menus or how to right click a mouse.

   When you learn Windows basics, you will have a rudimentary understanding of how to use almost everything. Most software applications today, even many Smart Phones, are Windows-based, meaning that they operate on the basic principles of Windows. That means if you know how to use Windows, you already know how to use almost everything. Alternatively, if you do not truly understand how to use Windows, you do not know how to use almost anything.

2. **Microsoft (MS) Outlook (or similar):** There is a whole lot more to Outlook than meets the eye. Also, learning to use Outlook will give you the essential understanding of email tools that you need. It will also help you in better understanding the internet and your CRM. Learn how to use an Outlook Calendar and Task Manager.

3. **MS Excel (Spreadsheets):** Start with the basics, but you need to know how to create and manipulate a simple spreadsheet and how to enter formulas. People may send you information in a spreadsheet and you have to know what to do with it. It is also very possible that you will need to compile information that you currently have on prospects and leads to upload into your new CRM. Chances are you have info on pieces of paper and files scattered all over the place, and the best way to begin to get that stuff together is to put it all into a spreadsheet that you can then *import* into your CRM.

You will need to understand how to configure columns and headers and how to set up a spreadsheet to match the upload configurations of the CRM.

4. **MS PowerPoint (Presentations):** You have to know how to quickly and efficiently create presentations and how to use them. Also, people will send you documents created in PowerPoint and you must know how to open and use those files.

5. **Facebook, Twitter, LinkedIn:** You may not like it, but these platforms have become major lead sources as well as viable methods to contact customers and prospects. You have to have a fair understanding of how to navigate these social media avenues.

6. **Smartphone Apps and Texting:** I am still amazed and often shocked at how many people today are unable to communicate via a cell phone besides traditional voice. All I can say is get it together, please.

Semester Review
CHAPTER 6
I = I.T.: Information Technology

---

1. CRM Software is a primary and mandatory component to operating as a professional and successful sales person in today's environment.

2. The primary purpose of your CRM is not for you to use as a calendar or for your company to keep tabs on you. The efficient and intentional use of CRM will dramatically increase your income.

3. The lack of CRM or good information management is one of the primary reasons of failure for most sales people.

4. An industry-specific CRM, preprogrammed with your sales process, activities and other sales metrics may be the best fit for you.

5. You must also get up to speed with other basic I.T. tools, such as Outlook, Excel, PowerPoint and Facebook.

Semester Assignments

1. If you do not have a company-provided CRM, you need to do some serious due diligence and begin researching CRM software tools. Keep your sales process in mind and investigate several. Get live/online demonstrations from the CRM makers, check out free trails, and talk to peers. Then get *extensive* training on the CRM you choose.

2. Get into other software programs as listed above and start using them. Get books, online training, go so classes or do whatever you have to do.

CHAPTER 7

C = C.A.R.E.:

I dare use the age-old axiom,

"People don't care how much you know,
until they first know how much you care."

When the customer can see that you truly have their best interest at heart and that you care more about their welfare and benefits than you do about making a commission, is when you will begin to see sales success beyond anything that you have ever imagined.

You need to care.

✓ You need to care about the prospect, the customer and the long-term client.

✓ You need to care about what you do.

✓ You need to care about your company.

✓ You need to care about your sales people.

✓ You need to care about your sales management.

✓ You need to care about your industry.

Some might say, "This is business, and I am not much of an emotional person. How can I care so personally about someone who, in most cases, is a total stranger?"

Understand that if you care about yourself, if you care about your family; then you *must* care about those things listed above.

Remember the lessons in Chapter 3, B: Believe. As I mentioned, there are many moral and ethical reasons why you should truly believe in what you sell. However, as I demonstrated, there are serious technical, tangible and financial reasons why you must believe wholeheartedly in what you sell and what you do.

The same holds true for caring. While there are a plethora of moral, ethical, spiritual and other intangible reasons to care; there are many more practical motives as well.

First, we are going get into some of the practical, financial and professional reasons to care. Then, we will wrap up everything with a visionary look at what it means to have a PhD in Sales.

The final semester of your education is on Customer (Patient) C.A.R.E. We will go over what it means to pull it all together and become a doctor; a Doctor of Selling, that is.

Caring = Cash

The bottom line is that caring for your prospective customers and clients pays off big time. You simply cannot and will not build a long-term, successful business without demonstrating exceptional customer care.

Here are few interesting facts for you:

☹ **96% of dissatisfied customers never complain**
("Understanding Customers" by Ruby Newell-Legner)
While you dance along thinking that everything is just fine and dandy, understand that most people don't tell you that they are unhappy. However...

☹ **91% of unhappy customers will never do business with you or your firm again.**
("Understanding Customers" by Ruby Newell-Legner)
That is real money that you will lose forever.

☹ **On average, a happy customer is worth about 10 times the amount of their initial purchase.**
(White House Office of Consumer Affairs)

That is real money in the bank. Clients that are happy and believe that you care for them, provide a significantly higher R.O.I. (Return On Investment).

⊗ **On average, a satisfied customer will tell 8 or 9 people, while a dissatisfied customer will tell 16 or more people.**
(American Express Survey, 2011)
Since I don't have factual statistics at the moment, I will not add anything to the above statement, however I believe the problem is exponentially worse today. Here, we are talking about dissatisfied customers who physically and personally talk to other people, in person or by telephone. Today however, you have to factor in things like a negative Facebook post, a Twitter Tweet or an Instgram, each of which have the ability of reaching hundreds, even thousands, of people.

According to a 2014 *Pew Research Center Survey*, the average person on Facebook has 338 Friends. Think about that for a moment.

One bad post about you and over 300 people can see it within moments. Then, imagine that only 10% of those people also *Likes* and *Shares* that post; and each of them also has over 300 Friends!

You cannot build a career with such skeletons lurking in your see-though closet. Remember what we talked about in the beginning of this book, on how today's consumer can have a dossier on you before you even show up for the appointment.   When that happens, you can bet those complaints and negative opinions and reviews about you will be in your virtual file folder.

You must protect and care for the customer because doing so protects your career! In sales, your reputation is your future; it is everything. Your reputation is also your company's future and image, as well as the image and representation of what you sell.

Remember, gone are the days where the buyer had to rely on what the sales person said. While you are running your mouth talking about how great you and your services are, the prospect is simultaneously looking you up on their smart phone!

I have literally tuned down sales, turned down commissions, because I felt the sale would somehow tarnish my reputation as a professional. One sale, no matter how big, no matter how much money is involved, is ever worth my good name!

I have been in sales, as you know, from the time I was 9 years old. That's a very long time and I can guarantee you that you will not find ONE person, not one person on this planet, that will tell you that John Landrine did a bad job or sold them a proverbial bill of goods.

From selling boxes of peanut brittle and chocolate thin mints, to vacuum cleaners, to outdoor signs, to software and I.T. services; there is not one single customer that I could not walk up to right now, this very day, who would not shake my hand and say, "John, it's good to see you."

Does that mean that in over 40 years of selling, that I do not have any unhappy customers? No, absolutely not. I am human and if you been in the world of selling for any length of time, then you know that there are some customers that you cannot satisfy, no matter what. So, yes, I have a few, extremely few, clients over the years who are less than content.

However, even they will tell you that I did not disappear on them, and that I did everything possible within my power and then some, to rectify the situation. Even they would say, "John it's good to see you."

Let me share one personal example of standing for doing what is right, even when it is unpopular and may cost you a sale.

What They Want Is Not Always What They Need

I was still a sales manager at Signtronix and we sold outdoor, internally lighted signs for independent businesses. While canvassing one day I came across a small strip mall and incredibly, was able to catch up with the owner of the property.

After giving him a super sales presentation, he agreed to let me replace all of the signs in the mall, which had about 10 currently occupied stores. All of the signs had to be uniform and the property owner said to let each storeowner know that he would pay for half of the cost of their sign. My working partner and I went to each store, doing presentations, designing renderings of each sign and closing sales.

Then we came to a small health food store, owned and operated by a sweet little lady I'll call Momma. Indeed, she could remind you of your grandmother.

I did the presentation as my partner drew up a rendering of the sign, which I presented to Momma. She really liked the design and the colors; however, she felt that something was missing.

Momma wanted us to put her store's telephone number on the sign. While, I was certain that I had explained issues like that during the presentation, I very patiently and empathically went over the reasons why putting the telephone number on the sign was not a good idea.

Yet, Momma began to insist. She felt that having her telephone number up there on her sign was not only necessary, but critical. Again, and still with patience and understanding, I explained that as experts in the sign business, nothing about the design we came up with was by accident. I explained that with the size of her sign, the letters had to be of a certain height to be legible from the distance needed for her store location. To add her phone number would mean that we would have to add an additional line to the sign, which would dramatically shrink everything so much, that it would make the whole sign unreadable from any distance.

The small shopping center sat back about 50 yards off the main street on the far side of the center's parking lot. Though the street had a significant amount of traffic, those cars needed to be able to see and recognize the businesses from the street, a good 150 to 200 feet away.

I pleaded with Momma to understand that people driving by on that street at 35 or 40 miles per hour were not going to be able to write down or even read her phone number.

Her business and every store in that center needed to broadcast to that busy street what businesses were in that center.

The shopping center also did not and could not have a marquee type entrance sign out near the street. Each of those stores needed a good, well-designed and effective storefront sign and the owner of the center realized that. Nevertheless, Momma would not give in.

She continued to insist we put her number on the sign and at this point, I had to refuse. Momma started yelling and screaming, which saddened and worried me, as she was not a young woman.

"You have to do what *I* want...it's *MY* sign!" She kept repeating.

"It may be *your* sign but it's *my reputation* and integrity." I honestly replied. "I cannot sell you something that will not do what it is intended to do."

When she realized that I was not going to budge and I began to get ready to leave without selling her a sign, she started crying!

"No! I want my sign!" She began appealing to my partner, hoping that he might listen to reason. "Please, please, why won't he just put my number on my sign? Whaaaaaa!!"

She was breaking my heart! But I still could not, with a clear conscience, grant her request.

The only possible way to do what she wanted would be to increase the size of her sign by almost 50%, which we could not do; the signs had to all be the same size and the size we were presenting was the only size that could fit on the storefronts.

Please understand; this was not me being some hard head or letting my ego or testosterone rule the day. I had seen this situation a dozen times before. I have seen what happens when an untrained sales rookie or a quick-buck artist does whatever the customer wants, just to make the sale. Here is exactly what would have happened if I had allowed sweet little Momma to have her way.

The Making of an Unhappy Customer

I go ahead and put Momma's phone number on the sign. On the rendering, on paper in her hand, it looks great. She loves her new sign and can't wait to get it.

A few weeks later, the sign arrives, comes off the truck and sits in a huge box on the floor awaiting installation. In the box, sitting on the floor, that sign looks fantastic and she is ecstatic.

They install the sign and she stands in the parking lot right beneath it, and it still looks beautiful.

However, on her way home that first day the sign is up, as she approaches the end of the parking lot and looks back at her new sign...horror sinks in.

The sign looks like postage stamp. She can't tell what it says at all. When she gets to the street, it's even worse; all she can see is a blur.

Now outraged, she seeks a refund, which we cannot grant. She wants to change the sign, which we also cannot do. The sign is vacuum-formed and molded into a Lexan surface. Once made, that's it. There is no such thing as painting over it. Friends and current customers that know Momma, tell her that they can't make out her new sign from any distance. Momma has spent a ton of money on a product that is essentially worthless and the only option to fix the problem would be for her to buy a brand new sign; which, by the way, her landlord would not pay for half of the second time around.

Now, Momma's only retribution is to bash me and my company to every person on earth that she can find.

I did not and would not do what I knew was not good for her or for me. I was ready to walk out of the door and lose that sale.

I also knew that walking out and not selling Momma a sign, could have meant that we would lose all of the sales in the complex! I am talking about throwing away thousands of dollars in commissions. Yet, I was ready to walk out and so was my partner.

For me, nothing was worth doing something that was not in her best interest. We would essentially be ripping Momma off and the result would be having her trash my reputation and firm's image for years.

Fortunately, we did not have to leave without the sale. Finally, my partner came up with an idea.

"How about this, Momma?" he suggested. "Let's go ahead and order the sign as we drew it up. Then, after the sign is installed, we will come back, and take a big wooden sign and paint your telephone number on it and hang it directly under your lighted sign. Could that work?"

"Sniff...sniff..." she managed. "I...I guess so..."

Well, 6 or 7 weeks later, we went back to the complex, visited all of the storeowners and looked for little sweet Momma. The moment we entered the store, she spotted us from behind the counter, dropped what was in her hands and charged at us.

Her feet nearly left the floor as she reached up and wrapped both of her arms around my neck, almost pulling me down, and began to hug and squeeze me so tight, I could hardly breathe.

"I've been waiting for you guys to come by!" She enthusiastically began. "I love my sign! Thank you so much! It is just wonderful! I am telling you, at least once every day; every single day, someone else comes in here and asks me if I just opened. When I tell them I been open for almost 3 years, they are shocked! They say that they been driving by here for years and never knew I was here! Some have even said that they had been *looking* for a health food store and been passing right by me! I can't believe it! Business is great! Thank you, thank you so much!"

By the time one of us was able to get a word in edgewise, my partner said, "That's great, Momma! We're so happy for you. And now we have come to go ahead and paint your phone number on something to put it up on your..."

"No...no, no..." Momma interrupted and said exactly this, as I will never forget it.

"It is not necessary to put my telephone number up there. You see, they all get my telephone number. They get my number printed on the sales receipt I give them for their purchase!"

I still get a little choked up whenever I tell that story.

Care about your customers. Care about what you do. Care about your reputation and be a consummate professional.

You have to *stand* for something. Become an expert, and then *advise* your customers on what is best for them. Don't just *sell* them something, advise them. Help them. Consult with them.

You have no doubt heard the old adage, "The customer is always right." I can tell you for a fact that such a thought is absurd. The customer is certainly not always right. It's not that the customer is always *wrong*; it is that they are usually not certain of what is right or wrong. That is why you are there. You are supposed to be the expert. You are supposed to advise them.

The Medical Doctor

In the beginning of this book, I used the example of a medical doctor for the sake of how much time, effort and money a professional should invest in his or her career.

If you are familiar with my work, heard me speak or been to any of my training seminars, then you know that for years I have compared what we do as professional sales people, to the job of a medical doctor. This is not because I admire medical doctors that much, but rather that the process of what we do is extremely similar to that of a physician.

In this final session, we will pull it all together so that you not only earn your PhD, but become a true Doctor of Sales.

Providing Customer (Patient) C.A.R.E.

As a true sales professional, you perform, or *should* perform, very much as a medical doctor. While you do not carry out the same duties and functions of a physician, you do operate with a similar process. That process for providing excellent customer or patient satisfaction is "C.A.R.E."

C.A.R.E.

C = Consult: Ask questions and do a thorough examination to uncover and expose areas of problems and pain.

A = Analyze: Examine all of the information and data to construct an appropriate solution.

R = Recommend: Recommend a remedy, a prescription, a solution to solve the problem.

E = Execute: Initiate the solution, begin the plan, close the sale, start the medication or schedule the operation immediately.

This is the plan that both you and the physician share. First, let's take a look at an overall generic process for the medical doctor.

The Doctor's Visit

C = Consult

I. Before meeting the patient, the doctor goes over the patient's medical information to become familiar with the patient and the medical concern.

II. The doctor then conducts an interview of sorts; asking the patient a lot of questions. As the doctor discovers new information, he or she asks more related questions and begins a cursory examination.

III. The doctor then performs a more comprehensive examination of the patient, performing all sorts of tests:

blood tests, urine samples, blood pressure, breathing tests, cardiac tests, etc.

A = Analyze

IV.   The doctor takes time and carefully goes over all of the results of the tests; analyzing all of the information and data until she is able to properly diagnose the problem, the pain or the cause of the condition.

R = Recommend

V.   Once the doctor has uncovered, exposed and identified the problem, she recommends a cure and prescribes a treatment plan.

E = Execute

VI.   Finally, the physician executes or initiates the plan and follows up with the patient to ensure they are well.

Again, that is a generic example, but that's how the process flows. The doctor asks a ton of questions and then does a thorough exam to uncover the problem, and finally prescribes the best treatment.

That is essentially what we do as sales professionals.

The Sales Call

C = Consult

I.   The sales professional reviews all of the available information about the lead before the appointment; visits the customer's website, checks out the company's suppliers and current pricing, etc.

II. The sales professional does an interview, asks questions and begins to uncover areas of problems and pain.

III. Then, the sales professional conducts a comprehensive discovery, conducting detailed inquiries and exposing all potential areas of pain.

A = Analyze

IV. The sales professional carefully analyzes all of the information and data and tailors a proposal that will address and solve the issues.

R = Recommend

V.   The sales professional presents the solution; prescribes the plan that will solve the problems, eliminate the pain or save the client money, etc.

E = Execute

VI.   Finally, the sales professional executes the solution by closing the sale and follows up to ensure the customer is satisfied.

You may feel that what you sell does not lend itself to being a *need,* or what you do does not actually solve a problem.

Perhaps what you sell is closer to something that people just like and want rather than something that they need.

You sell vacation time-shares and people do not really *need* a time-share. Or you sell luxury cars that could never solve a problem for anyone.

Keep two things in mind:

1.   Understand that even a desire is a type of need. The person certainly feels as though they need to quench that desire. Hence, filling that desire is solving a problem and filling a need. The situation then becomes helping the prospective customer get the best value and the best solution available.

2. Remember the very first step in the BASICs, the B. You must believe. If you do not believe that your time-shares or your luxury cars are the best on the market and will satisfy your clients' desires, then you should not sell them.

You are the doctor. You are the expert who is supposed to HELP the client get what they want and need. With that thought in mind, let's go back to my story about Momma.

As the doctor, I knew what was best for the patient. I knew what the patient really needed, whether she knew it or not. I knew better than the patient did as to what was best for her.

Isn't that the way it is with the doctor? Doesn't your doctor know what is better for you than you usually do? (If you answered no, then unless you are a medical professional, I would consider a new doctor.)

For me to allow that customer to have what she wanted, what *she* thought was right, would have been tantamount to medical malpractice. It would have been selling malpractice!

Hold on! Someone is thinking, "Wouldn't it had been best to sell Momma *something,* rather than leave without making a sale at all?

John R. Landrine

True, with her telephone number up there like she wanted, the sign would not have been as effective, but wouldn't it have been better than nothing?"

No! It was not a question of being 80% effective vs. being 100%. It was the difference between 100% and 0%!

Imagine about this…

You have a toothache and it's a bad one. It started slowly a couple of days ago and now it is so painful that you had to get an emergency appointment to see the dentist.

You don't know what the problem is, all you know is that you need to stop the pain.

The dentist gives you a quick examination and then asks you something like this,

"Okay, so what would you like me to do?"

How would you react to that?

You might reply with something like, "What do you mean, what do I want you to do? You're the dentist; you tell me!"

The dentist tells you, "Well, I believe that the customer is always right and I always want a satisfied customer so, I will do whatever you wish. I can drill a couple of the teeth in the back.

I can drill and maybe put on a crown. I can even do a root canal, if you like. I can also pull a few teeth. In fact, we have extractions on sale this week. Which ones would you like me to yank out?"

I imagine you'd be out of the door by then.

Yet, another way to look at this is, what if the dentist or doctor took your suggestion and treated you according to what *you* thought was best.

The dentist's examination shows that you have an infection deep down in the root of a tooth. She knows that the only solution is to do a root canal, get down in there and clear out that infection. Medication will not help, nor will yanking out the tooth or putting in a filling. The dentist prescribes the root canal, followed by a filling or a crown.

However, you know best. You are certain that if she would just put in a filling, you will be fine, plus you really don't want to come up with the big co-pay for a root canal and you insist that the dentist do as you wish.

Switch sides for a moment, and you be the dentist. If that were your patient, would you do what he or she wanted? Sure, the pain would go away momentarily, but you know that it would return with a vengeance within a few days. Not only would the pain be much worse, but the patient now risks gum disease, blood poisoning or worse.

I know those examples seem extreme, but you need to realize that they are not. As a sales professional, remember the importance of what you do. You have to do what is right and what is best. This is serious. What you do is serious.

Learn all there is to learn about what you do. Become a genuine expert, and then teach, advise and help your customers get what they want and truly need.

The Doctor and Patient Want the Same Thing

As a professional, your goal should be the same as the customer's. The physician's ultimate goal should be to help the patient be made well, stay well and to do so as expeditiously as possible.

As a sales doctor, your ultimate goal should likewise be to help the customer be made well, stay well and to do so expeditiously.

With that said, are there doctors who have motives that are more selfish? Are there doctors who do what they can to prolong the patient's treatment, prescribe medications and procedures that are unnecessary and do what they can to put more money in their pockets?

Of course there are! And it is clear how those few have severally tarnished the image of the medical profession; artificially inflating the cost of medical care and have blatantly violated the near sacred Hippocratic Oath, specifically in which they are to *"first do no harm."*

Similarly, there are sales people who do the same in the world of selling.

Once again, does this mean that a doctor or a sales person should not seek to earn lots of money? No. What it means is that neither the doctor nor the sales person should ever look to make money *at the expense of the patient or customer.*

The doctor and the patient want the same thing; they are on the same side.

However, many sales people feel that they and the prospect are on opposite sides of the fence. For most sales people, the sales process is more of a battle, a fight to see who wins.

If the sales person wins, they close the sale. If they do not close the sale, then the prospect wins. It is from this outdated way of thinking that you get such thoughts as *winning the sale.*

You hear sales people talk about winning or losing the sale all the time. The sales interaction is one where someone must win and someone must lose.

This archaic way of thinking creates an adversarial relationship between the sales person and the consumer.

As a true professional, as a doctor, as a doctor with a specialized PhD, a MD-PhD, you must understand that selling is never a WIN-LOSE situation. Selling is always a WIN-WIN or a LOSE-LOSE proposition. You and the prospect are on the same side and it is not a fight.

You committed earlier to only sell something that you wholeheartedly believe in, something that you are certain is best for your customer. You honestly believe that what you sell will help the customer. If that is true, then when you make the sale, how can you feel that the customer lost?

If you go to the doctor with a broken arm and the doctor fixes it, did you lose?

> **Selling is never a WIN-LOSE situation. Selling is always a WIN-WIN or a LOSE-LOSE proposition.**

If what you sold was the best thing for the customer and it helped the customer, then how could that customer be a loser?

On the other hand, if you do not close the sale, then the customer did not get something that was best for them. If you do not make the sale, the customer failed to receive something that would have helped him or her.

If you do not make the sale, then you failed to solve a problem for the client; you did not help the customer and they are still suffering.

How in the world can anyone say that the customer won in such an instance?

When the surgeon loses a patient on the operating table and the patient dies...

Who won?

You and the prospective buyer are on the same side and want the same thing. You both either win together or lose together!

When you make the sale, both you and the customer win. When you do not make the sale, both you and the customer lose.

When you do not make the sale, you have failed to help the customer. When you do not make the sale, you did not do your job. When you do not make the sale, it is possible you are guilty of malpractice.

Semester Review
CHAPTER 7
C = C.A.R.E.

---

1. Caring equals more money in your pocket and ensures a more successful, solid sales career. You must care about and for your customers and your career.

2. Your reputation, your good name is your future and you only have one. You must do whatever is necessary to do what is right. Never leverage your tomorrow for a commission today. To do so is to step over dollars to pick up pennies.

3. C.A.R.E. Embrace the process of an MD: Consult, Analyze, Recommend and Execute.

4. You and the prospect are on the same side and want the same thing. You both want to help the prospect solve his or her problem. You both want the prospect to get what is best for them.

5. Selling is never a WIN-LOSE situation. Selling is always a WIN-WIN or LOSE-LOSE proposition. When you make the sale, both you and the customer win.

When you do not close the sale, both you and the prospect lose. When you do not make the sale, you have failed the customer. When you do not make the sale, you have failed to do your job. When you do not make the sale, you may be guilty of malpractice.

Demand excellence of yourself and accept nothing less!

Follow the BASICs. It is not easy and requires a whole lot of work. Some of you may have months to go to get there, while some people may already have enough time invested. Then, for others, it may take you many years to arrive at the PhD level in sales.

However, if you will:

- ✓ Believe in what you sell
- ✓ Ask for the order with conviction, use the
- ✓ Science of Selling, maximize the use of
- ✓ Information Technology and truly
- ✓ Care about your customer and your profession; you will see professional, financial and personal success that even most brain surgeons cannot match!

You have the most important job in the world.
Raise your level of expertise.
Elevate your level of professionalism.

Earn a PhD in Sales!

God Bless You!

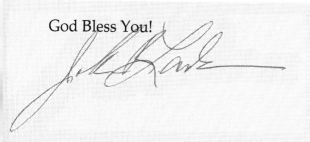

Made in the USA
Columbia, SC
20 October 2022

69785182R00133